Village Japan

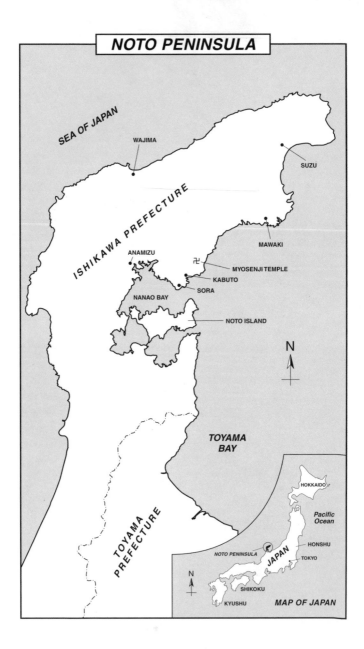

Village Japan

Everyday Life in a
Rural Japanese Community

Malcolm Ritchie

Charles E. Tuttle Company
Rutland, Vermont & Tokyo, Japan

Published by Charles E. Tuttle Publishing,
an imprint of Periplus Editions (HK) Ltd.

LCC Card No. 98-89152
ISBN 0-8048-2121-6

First edition, 1999

Printed in Singapore

Distributed by:

USA **Charles E. Tuttle Co., Inc.**
Airport Industrial Park
RR1 Box 231-5
North Clarendon, VT 05759
Tel: (802) 773-8930
Fax: (802) 773-6993

Japan **Tuttle Shokai Ltd.**
1-21-13 Seki
Tama-ku, Kawasaki-shi
Kanagawa-ken 214-0022, Japan
Tel: (81) (44) 833-0225
Fax: (81) (44) 822-0413

Southeast Asia
Berkeley Books Pte Ltd.
5 Little Road #08-01
Singapore 536983
Tel: (65) 280 3320
Fax: (65) 280 6290

Tokyo Editorial Office:
2-6, Suido 1-chome,
Bunkyo-ku, Tokyo 112-0005, Japan

Boston Editorial Office:
153 Milk Street, 5th Floor
Boston, MA 02109, USA

Singapore Editorial Office:
5 Little Road #08-01
Singapore 536983

◆ Contents ◆

*This book is dedicated to
the people of Sora*

◆ Preface ◆

My wife, Masako, and I had decided to return to Japan, where we had previously lived in Tokyo for five years, hoping to find somewhere in the countryside where we could support ourselves by doing translation work. In the event, a chance meeting with a young Japanese couple, the Yokos, who had come to study in Britain for a year, led us to a remote farming/fishing village on the Noto Peninsula on the Japan Sea coast.

Initially, on our arrival in Noto, we stayed in the house of Mr. Yoko's mother in the village of Kanami while we searched the area for an empty house that might be suitable to rent. One evening Mr. Yoko returned home to say that he had heard of an empty house in the neighboring village of Sora and that he would take us to look at it the following day.

The next morning after breakfast, Mr. Yoko drove us the four kilometers to Sora, through the village main street to a point where the road crossed a bridge with vermilion railings. There we took a turning to the left and stopped outside a house just a few yards from the bridge. The house stood at the apex of a triangle formed by the confluence of two small rivers that flowed close to either side of it and came together just a few yards from its front door, between it and the bridge. A small footbridge gave access to the house across the river that ran between the house and the road.

Just as we were getting out of the car, a very small man

appeared suddenly, as if from nowhere, and wandered across the road toward us. He was about four feet six inches in height, with a swarthy skin and an unshaven chin. As he approached us, he held his head back slightly in order to look up at us. His walk was more a kind of shuffle, and he held the branch of a tree in his right hand as a walking stick.

I bowed and said, "*Konnichiwa*" (Good day), and he returned my bow with "*Konnichiwa*. Who are you? I don't know you." His curiosity seemingly satisfied, he turned his back and shuffled away in the direction of a large dilapidated house beside the vermilion bridge.

At the time, I wondered how to interpret his greeting and worried, having been told how conservative these villages were, how he might react on finding that a foreigner was going to live almost opposite his house. On our moving in, however, I was soon relieved of any such apprehension because Mr. Fukada, who was eighty-three, and known locally by his given name as Old Man Gonsaku, became a close neighbor and friend. In fact, for me he was the genius loci, with more than a little trickster in his nature. A man who seemed to live in his own time/space, ignoring the more conventional attitudes and habits of his neighbors and often perplexing them with his own. He had, for example, a predilection for going to the lavatory al fresco, although his house was furnished with the traditional dry lavatory. The site of his choice was a few yards in front of his own house, at the crossroads between the main village street and the turnoff from the vermilion bridge to the road on which our own house was situated. Actually, the spot he had chosen was directly opposite my workroom window, and in the spring and summer months I was to be frequently disturbed away from my desk by the sounds of altercation as he was berated where he squatted by someone passing on a bicycle on their way to or from their fields or from the back of a tractor and trailer. He always seemed to have a ready rejoinder, which he delivered with whatever else he was depositing at the time, without adjustment to either his position or his dropped trousers or indeed his determination to continue whatever he was engaged in.

Old Man Gonsaku's presence is frequent throughout the pages of this book, as indeed it was throughout the days, and sometimes nights, of our sojourn in Sora. And here he is, already at the beginning of the book, much in the same way that he appeared on our first visit to the house we were to live in for the next two and a half years.

This book is not intended as a sociological, anthropological, historical, or any other kind of study. Rather it is a collection of anecdotes, encounters, conversations, and thoughts that I recorded in notebooks and on tapes during the period that we lived in Sora. This being the case, I have not set out to produce an in-depth portrait of life in a Japanese village but to bring a miscellany of subjects, people, and places, which interested, affected or concerned me at the time, briefly into focus. As is often the case in situations like this, there are many stories that cannot be told for a variety of reasons, not least because they involve the lives of others from whom I do not have the permission to recount them, or they fall outside the territory covered by this book. There is no mention, for example, of the Hanshin Earthquake or the capture of the Aum Shinrikyō "doomsday" cult members, both events we were well aware of at the time—the earthquake having been felt in the village, three members of the cult discovered hiding in a house not far from where we lived, and we, ourselves, having been stopped and questioned during the search. While one or two of the stories extend beyond, and in a couple of cases far beyond, the boundaries of Sora, it was Sora that remained the home base, both from a physical as well as an emotional and psychological orientation.

When you pass a large, old Japanese house, often all you can see of it are glimpses above its walls, between the bamboo slats of a fence, or behind the wooden grill of a gate—sections of roof, brief views of garden, the hump of an ornamental rock, the carved window of a stone lantern, or maple leaves against the sky. Like Japanese haiku or Zen ink painting, it is in that which is not seen or stated but only suggested that evokes a profound resonance within us, that ignites the imagination.

Whilst I can in no way approach or claim that kind of depth in either effect or meaning in this collection of anecdotes and writings, I should like to use the analogy to explain the form and texture of this book. What I have attempted to do is to suggest something of the experience of living in Sora, without covering every aspect of Japanese village life or necessarily providing a linear continuity of narrative to make a complete story. I have always preferred the diary or journal form to that of the novel or short story, as it seems to present a greater fidelity or authenticity to the way in which everyday life actually feels in retrospect.

Originally, my intention was to write quite a different sort of book. I had the idea to write a kind of "calendar" of the cycle of Shinto and Buddhist festivals and events and of how they are woven into the agricultural and domestic rhythms of rural village life. The more involved I became in the everyday lives and concerns of our neighbors, however, the more I realized the material for a very different kind of book. This presented a problem in that I had to be careful not to treat my daily life and experiences merely as material for a book per se. If I had kept this intention to the fore, so that it simply became my reason for being in the village, then it would have intruded upon my relationships with my neighbors and my life there. At times, of course, it was necessary to make specific inquiries and interviews with the self-appointed historians of Sora and one or two neighboring villages. At other times I encountered a different stratum of information in the memories of the unselfconscious custodians of the village's past, like Old Man Gonsaku and the women of the village.

Coupled with the above difficulty, which lies along that border that exists between living each day as integrated as is possible for a foreigner in what is usually a very closed community and the inevitable objectifying of it which results from making "use" of it, was the difficulty of using a camera. I have always had an ambivalence toward, and what I suppose is a primitive suspicion of, the camera. Somehow, I have always felt that there is some kind of theft analogous to a "stealing of the soul." Perhaps this damage is in the way it violates the moment. Maybe it is because we are incapable of truly living in the moment that we feel we have to try to "steal" it in some way. And it seemed significant to me that on my first photographic trip with my new expensive Japanese camera I should have dropped it on a rock, damaging it.

I am neither a natural cameraman nor a comfortable photographic subject myself. It is my shyness with the camera, and the feeling of intrusion it creates, that is the reason for the absence of photographs of people in their unguarded moments, in their homes or fields, at their domestic and workaday lives. Although I did obviously use the camera, I still have not resolved this dilemma for myself.

As the material began to collect on tapes and scraps of paper around the house, so it began to suggest a form, albeit amorphous, of an elegiac nature, with the realization that a whole way of life and natural wisdom was vanishing with the demise of the present, aged generation of these villages. Not only what was still a rural peasant life for most of our neighbors but, I believe, still lived at the very birth-ground of Japanese culture itself. And what was to become an increasingly uncomfortable but obvious fact was the realization that it is the industrial-technological materialism of the West, the West's cultural carcinogens, that the Japanese so eagerly embrace, which has destroyed the fabric and spirit of a once great culture, and is even now consuming the remaining cultures of Asia.

Before commencing further, it is necessary to locate Sora more precisely and to sketch out some of the main features of life and culture in a rural Japanese village so that what follows in the stories will make sense.

◆ Acknowledgments ◆

It goes without saying that the writing of this book would have proved impossible without the presence of my wife, Masako, on so many of the journeys I made, and who so patiently untangled and explained many of the complexities of Japanese language and customs. Thanks must also go to Mr. and Mrs. Yoko, for without our having met them, and their generous suggestion that we should visit them in their native land of Noto, we would never have had the opportunity of living in Sora. And most importantly, gratitude goes to Mr. and Mrs. Sawada for allowing us to rent what had been Mr. Sawada's mother's house in Sora.

The fact that this book is published by the Charles E. Tuttle Company is due to the guidance of our good friend Shinji Takagi, a fine architect and custodian of the "old ways."

Finally, thanks goes to Graham Chappell and Andrew Grazier at Arran Graphics & Computers for their invaluable help in times of need.

PART ONE

◆ Introduction ◆

Sora Area

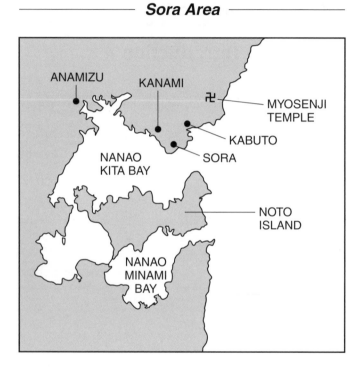

◆ Northern Noto

The Noto Peninsula resembles a dorsal fin sticking out from the middle of the back of the main island of Honshū into the Japan Sea. The peninsula is part of Ishikawa prefecture, and its northern part curves eastward at an almost forty-five degree angle to its southern part. This means that one side of the peninsula faces the Japan Sea, while the other curves in toward the direction of the mainland. Due to this, these two coasts are known as the "outer coast" and the "inner coast," respectively. The outer is wild and rugged, while the inner is mild and sheltering. Hence, these very different environments are sometimes referred to as "Father" and "Mother," and the character of the villages along these coasts is, accordingly, quite different. It is on the "inner coast," in the bay created by the crook of the curve of the peninsula, which contains Noto Island (Notojima), where the village of Sora is situated. This inner coastline looks toward the Tateyama Mountains across the expanse of Nanao Bay, which is formed between the curve in the peninsula and the mainland.

The northern area of Noto is often referred to as "Far Noto," and the nature and energy of the place is best expressed in the words of an old peddler's song: "Noto is a gentle place; even the earth is so."

A slangy term that describes another aspect of the energy on this peninsula is *totoraku* (literally, "father's ease"), because traditionally the women do most of the work! Not only do they care for home and family but they also farm, and often hold a job either within the village itself or somewhere nearby. Their days begin very early and end long after everyone else has gone to bed. And when the men are socializing at home, the wife is very often excluded from the table, while being expected to cater to every whim of her husband and his guests. This extraordinary feminine energy and forbearance was one of the first things that impressed me when we arrived. It permeates the entire fabric of life in the villages and the surrounding fields.

An epithet often applied to the areas of country facing the Japan Sea is "the back of Japan," while the Pacific side is called the "front," because it faces toward the West. From the end of the Tokugawa period, around 1867, the West was perceived as more advanced than either China or the Korean Peninsula, both of which had previously been the main direction of trade and played, of course, a major seminal role in the development of Japanese culture.

It is because of this area's present remoteness and the fact that it has largely been ignored in the modern era that it has become the repository of a very rich and ancient culture, which has only in recent times begun to be eroded by twentieth-century consumerism—the enemy of all holistic cultures. The fact that Noto is only now becoming of interest to scholars and writers is, unfortunately and depressingly, an indicator of its imminent demise—the "culture vultures" circling over it in its death throes. And here I am, I suppose, sharing these same carrion-scented thermals!

◆ Sora Village

The village of Sora stands within the sheltering crook of the peninsula on a small inlet into which the confluence of the two small rivers that passed our house flows and which opens into the bay where Noto Island is located. The village itself faces south across this sheltered bay and toward the island, Nanao Bay, and the Tateyama Mountains beyond.

There are no services with regard to bus, taxi, or railway station in or near the village, since the railway makes a detour around it. Taxis have to drive in from the town of Anamizu, some sixteen kilometers away, and most of the aged inhabitants either walk or ride bicycles to and from neighboring villages.

The village consists of about eighty houses. On one side it faces the sheltered waters of the bay, which are the fishing grounds of the village's tiny fishing fleet of small boats. And at its back are densely forested hills that rise up like lumpy islands out from the small, flattened valleys formed by the rice fields. On some areas of the higher ground, the trees have been cleared to make way for tobacco fields and the occasional chicken or dairy farm, owned by incomers to the area according to the vagaries of the agricultural policies of successive governments. Here are the remains of several derelict chicken farms, with the haunted ambience of abandoned concentration camps.

At one end of the village is the Shinto shrine, set atop a small wooded hill, standing just back from the village itself. At the other end of the village is an ancient Buddhist temple of the Shingon sect. It stands at the top of a flight of stone steps with its back to the forest, just across the road from the water's edge, commanding a view across the bay to the sacred mountain of Tateyama. Both provide the poles of spiritual focus that form the village's religious life.

◆ The Name "Sora"

When we first moved into Sora, on my inquiry someone told us that Sora was named after one of the pupils of the great haiku poet Matsuo Bashō. Sora had been Bashō's traveling companion on his famous journey, described through linked prose and haiku in his famous *Narrow Road to the Deep North*. Sora was supposed to have stayed in a house in the area at some time during his life.

Of course, this idea greatly appealed to me, until we discovered that it had no basis in fact and that a study of the characters forming the name suggests "a place in front of a cliff." The most likely possibility offered, however, is that it was named by a local samurai family who, moving to the area from a nearby village called Asora, named the place they resettled "Sora." There does appear to be some historical evidence for this, but it remains speculative. No one we asked really seemed to know.

The reaction of many of the people we met in local towns and other villages, when they inquired as to where we lived, was one of surprise and often shock. "Sora?!" Often adding, "How inconvenient!" They simply could not understand why an educated Tokyo-born woman and a Western man would want to live in such a poor, remote village with no nearby "cultural center." What they expressed was the fact that they failed to recognize the very importance of villages like Sora.

As portrayed in myth, folk, and fairy tales, and well understood in alchemy and psychotherapy, it is often that which is despised, overlooked, and ignored wherein lies the greatest treasure. To me, this is precisely what Sora represents. In spite of all the great storehouses of Japanese culture in the cities of Japan, including those that are synonymous with the culture itself, such as Kyoto and Nara (both ancient capitals), it is in Sora, and in the little places like it elsewhere in Japan, that what I believe to be the last remnants of true living Japanese culture remain. Not as a quaint anachronism in a largely Westernized mainline consumer society, but a place where it is still ordinary everyday life—a way of living, still firmly rooted in the Japanese soil and under the tutelage of its ancient gods, and not a comfortable cul-de-sac of cultural and religious lip-service.

The tragedy is that it is now autumn in these villages, with the penumbra of the shadow of winter already fast

descending. And with the demise of the present generation of elders, when that winter's snows have melted so
too will have most of the traces of an albeit hard way of
life, but with it all the beauty, skills, knowledge, wisdom
and faith of a noble people.

This is in no way to romanticize a life of frequent pri-
vation—the very conditions of which, in fact, temper it
physically and spiritually—but to recognize a life filled
with suffering, happiness, humor, and gratitude for that
very kind of life, and a meaning that transcends the very
concept of the word, wherein the meaning is in the life
lived. This is a way of living that we have largely forgotten
and the "meaning" of which we desperately need to find
ways to reconnect with, in lives which have become, and
continue to be, increasingly trivialized and disoriented.

Often, visiting the homes and work places of the old
people of the village, I was struck by the difference
between aesthetics born out of necessity, practicality,
and aging through generations of use—where the objects
that make up and define the living / working environment
are evidence of a continuity of living, often hard and poor
from the perspective of today's standards and values—
and those found in the places we now generally inhabit.

◆ The House

Most of the houses in the village, with a few exceptions,
are old houses. These are traditionally built of cedar-
wood frames between which are lathes of bamboo tied
with rice straw. The lathes are plastered with a three-layer
mixture of clay and rice straw to form the house walls.
This is a more sophisticated version of the familiar
European wattle-and-daub technique.

For the first layer, rice straw is chopped into small
pieces and then mixed with clay and left for a year to
soften the straw. After a year, it is reworked and spread

over the lathes and left to dry. The next layer consists of very finely cut straw mixed with clay that has a little sand added to it. Finally, a layer of sandy clay, with local color added and bound with a glue obtained by boiling *funori* (a type of seaweed), is smoothed over the first two layers. Many houses then have these walls clad with cedar weatherboards.

In the old days, all the houses were thatched. While examples still remain scattered throughout the peninsula, all the houses in Sora are now tiled. Examples of the original old tiles are still borne by many of the roofs in the village, and they have a natural warmth in their color and form, compared to the mass-produced tiles of today.

The houses are mainly two-storied, and the living area is partitioned into separate tatami-floored rooms by the use of paper-covered sliding doors called *karakami* (or *fusuma*). This provides a versatile space in which the size and number of rooms can be changed according to the needs of the moment. For example, in the event of gatherings and parties the *karakami* can be either opened or removed altogether to provide a space almost as large as the ground floor. This does mean, however, that there is little privacy living in a traditional Japanese house.

At least one room in the house will feature a *tokonoma*, an alcove in which a scroll depicting a religious subject or the appropriate seasonal scene will be hung, with perhaps a work of art or a flower arrangement beneath it.

As each family is affiliated to both the local Shintō shrine as well as a Buddhist temple of one sect or another (not necessarily the local temple), one will find both Shintō household shrines and a Buddhist household altar in the same house.

The Shintō household shrine or *kamidana* (literally, "god shelf") enshrining the household gods (*kami*) is traditionally located either in a room near the entranceway (*genkan*) or the main living room. There will also be a small shrine in the kitchen, for the kitchen gods.

The Buddhist household altars (*butsudan*) in the countryside are usually very large and elaborate and because of the craftsmanship involved cost many thousands of dollars. Usually a special room is devoted to the *butsudan*, the design of which, and the image enshrined therein, will vary according to the sect to which the family belongs.

Entering a Japanese house at ground level, there is a small vestibule (*genkan*) from which one steps up a step and into the house proper. It is here that one removes one's outdoor shoes and, stepping up into the house, dons a pair of slippers, at least as far as the threshold of a tatami room, where even the slippers will be abandoned as they are only worn on the hard floors of the house.

Traditionally, a country house would have had at least one room in which there was an open square-shaped fireplace set into the floor, called an *irori*, over which cooking would be done, and around which the family and guests would sit. Generally speaking, this room would have no floor above it, and the smoke would exit through a vent in the roof.

Sadly these days, although some still retain a working *irori*, in one room of most old houses in the village there will be a dip in the tatami, rather like the shallow depression left by a pauper's grave. This is the site of an *irori* that has been abandoned and covered over with tatami. The main reason for this is that there are now much safer ways of heating and cooking in buildings that are very prone to the risk of fire.

The disappearance of hearths in Japan, however, as in other parts of the world, apart from any environmental considerations or safety precautions, is also, I believe, a symbolic indication of the direction that our sophisticated, so-called civilized cultures are taking us. It has always struck me that the word "hearth" looks as though it is composed of the two words "heart" and "earth," and the world over, the fire used to be the heart of the home and was originally built simply on the earth (Scotland and

Ireland often burned earth in the form of peat). These days we are forgetting both heart and earth in our haste toward haste.

◆ The Storehouse (Kura)

Apart from barns and outhouses, it is common for a house to have a special storehouse (*kura*) close by, or sometimes adjoining it. These buildings have a distinctive design and structure of their own and somewhere on their exterior (a shutter or gable end) bear the family crest. The *kura* is used for storing furniture and domestic items that are not in use during a particular season. Traditionally, furnishings, such as sitting cushions (*zabuton*), futons and covers, *karakami*, pottery, lacquer ware, hanging scrolls, pictures, etc., along with seasonal clothing, will be changed according to the time of year. The furnishings, decorations, and even eating utensils will reflect colors, images, and themes of the seasonal landscape and farming activities outside the house. As in the winter, materials will tend to be heavier and more solid, to create a feeling of warmth within the house, and at the same time often carry images of winter; so in the summer, things will tend to be made of materials light in terms of both weight and color in order to create a general feeling of coolness and airiness during the hot, humid months. At the same time, different utensils and furnishings might be used for special occasions—weddings, funerals, etc.— and need to be stored when not in use. Foodstuffs, such as rice and miso, are also stored in the *kura*, which is built with thick walls of clay or stone that maintain a stable temperature and humidity throughout the year's seasonal extremes. Of prime importance, of course, is the fact that they are fireproof.

In addition to the *kura*, in a village like Sora where each household is engaged in either farming or fishing, or often both, there is also at least one barn or outhouse attached or in close proximity to the house. In the case of our own house, there was a barn adjoining the back of the house, with access to it internally from the kitchen, as well as from the outside.

Up until the fifties, each household kept a bullock which was used for a variety of tasks throughout the agricultural calendar. Since then, farmers began to buy gasoline-engined cultivators and, later, small versatile tractors. These tractors consist of an engine on two wheels, with long handlebars for steering and on which the controls are mounted. This two-wheeled tractor is made stable by a variety of combinations—tractor and trailer, tractor and cultivator, and so on.

The bullock and the cadence of its movement—the rhythm of which impressed itself not only physically in the shaping of fields and tracks but also on the temporal frame of work and life—its body temperature, its smell, and voice like the working horse of Britain, has vanished from Noto and the rest of Japan. But now and then, a hint or shadow can be detected in a neglected byre-end of a barn, the grease on the side of a doorway or wall, the warm patina on an old hitching-place, or glimpsed in the minds of the aged in the warmth of his or her voice when reminiscing around the fire or beside the stove on a winter's night.

◆ The Bath (Furo)

Most of our neighbors still heated their baths by burning wood. Some of these tubs were made of cast iron with the fire built directly beneath them. This entailed the installation of a wooden pallet on the bottom of the tub to prevent the bather's lower body from getting burned. But the more traditional types of tub were constructed of cypress wood, with a section built into the bath, incorporating a cast-iron firebox into which the wood was placed for heating the water.

Between 4:30 and 5:00 in the afternoon, depending on the season, when villagers returned from the fields, and before they had their evening meal, the first clouds of blue smoke from their baths would drift between the houses, or lift like a spirit-form of the tree that the wood had once been, into the sky, perfuming the village.

Passing by a house, you would hear the distinctive sounds of water being lifted from the tub and poured over the bather's body with a wooden scoop or plastic bowl, and the "clop" sound as it was replaced on the floor after the ablutions were completed. The bather then stepped into the tub to soak. These sounds would echo and be magnified by the bare walls of the bathroom, as would the voice, often sweetened with saké, of one of our neighbors, the headman on a late summer's night in the bath after a night's drinking.

Regrettably, our own bath had been converted so that the water was heated by a kerosene-fired heater in a system separate from the bathroom and located in the barn, while the kerosene tank was secured to the outside wall just below the window of the bathroom.

In the old days in the village, only certain houses possessed a bathroom, so that those families that had none were invited to bathe in a neighbor's house. In some houses, as many as forty people might have bathed in one tub of an evening.

Generally, the bathroom floor is tiled or is made of concrete with a wooden deck. Sometimes the tub is sealed into the floor which has a drain, and often in older bathrooms there is a pit beneath the tub where a drain is situated. It was in just such a pit beneath the tub in an old house we lived in, in Tokyo, that I discovered a dead rat. The smell had been getting progressively worse each time we entered the house over the period of a week, until the molecules it was borne on began to describe precisely the shape of its origin and its location. One evening I looked beneath the tub with the aid of a torch, and there it was, at the far end. I cut two long, thin pieces of bamboo from our tiny garden and, using them like chopsticks, tried to extricate the corpse, which had by now, in the warmth of spring weather, decomposed and was merely assuming its former shape and offered nothing substantial to take hold of. It simply became rat puree at the ends of the bamboo! I finally had to flush it out by emptying the water from the tub, which filled the entire pit before it reached the drain, where its escape became impeded by fur and small pieces of bone that I had to remove by hand.

The stench had become so powerful during this operation—its last molecular onslaught being augmented by the water—that it became indelibly imprinted on my olfactory processes and associated with the bathroom scent of soap. For weeks afterward, each time I came to bathe it was as though I soaped my body with the corpse of the rat!

◆ The Toilet (Benjo)

The toilet in our house was a traditional Japanese *benjo*; that is, basically just a hole in the floor that accessed to a large dark cavern beneath the house over which one crouched, not unlike lavatories in many other parts of the world. And since we owned no rice field on which to use the contents as fertilizer, it had to be emptied by a local firm at regular intervals, usually according to the number of people visiting the house. Once it was emptied, the heavy dark smell that emerged from it and permeated the house, and probably our clothes as well, gave way to a strange scent like a bouquet of ozone, and the first turds of the new cycle echoed like hymn books being dropped in a cathedral.

This ecclesiastical image is not entirely out of place, as I remember once, when I was staying in a Zen temple, that it was my duty to clean the *benjo*. This task entailed scraping the day's feces from a wooden chute just below the hole into the pit. This operation was performed with the help of a large wooden spatula with a prayer written on its handle and was considered an important spiritual practice.

On the occasion of having our *benjo* emptied for the first time after moving in, added to the expected contents it was discovered to contain six pairs of slippers! This find, from then on, seemed to endow the space below the house with the powers of some lower-world purgatory.

After some months, we learned that the Korean family firm who owned the vacuum truck used in this operation also ran the best restaurant in the local town of Anamizu. Taking care of both ends of the process seemed to make perfect sense. It reminded me of a Vietnamese restaurant that we once discovered in Tokyo called "Mai Dung."

◆ Rice Fields (Tambo)

In early spring as the air gets warmer, the rice fields are flooded in preparation for planting. Suddenly, the landscape becomes filled with light, as if the land was laid out with mirrors reflecting the sky and the forested hills, opening up the earth and doubling the world. At night, the fields become holes in the ground to another sky beyond, which is filled with a chorus of croaking stars. And as early summer draws up the green shoots from the water, so some of those stars, too, rise from that other sky and fly as galaxies of fireflies.

In spring, the airspace above the village becomes filled with the excited cries of swallows flying back and forth over the roofs, as though dowsing, refamiliarizing themselves with its topography and relocating the sites of the previous year's nests. The village streets fill with the noise of tractors and people on foot, coming and going back and forth between their homes and their fields.

These first few weeks are a time when bodies that had been housebound all winter, or at least far less active, suffer from the sudden intense physical activity.

Whereas at one time all the processes involved in the cultivation of rice were done by hand, except for those like ploughing where the bullock was used, today ploughing and planting are most often mechanized. In some of the smaller fields around the village, however, the work is still done by hand.

The bodies of the old people, particularly the women, bear witness to decades of hard work in the fields. It is a very common sight in country areas to see the backs of old women that are so permanently bent from a lifetime of stooping to plant, weed, and harvest that their spines, from the waist up, are horizontal with the ground. They have to support themselves on sticks or on infant's buggies, which they wheel before them, often with their shopping or produce from their fields on board.

I never failed to be moved by the way the women spoke of their love for the land on which they worked and lived in a reciprocal relationship—a relationship that had often given them hardship and pain, and shaped it into their bodies. They did not speak of this love per se, it was simply in the language they used when talking of the earth, the plants, or the seasons, or in the manner in which a woman farmer would unconsciously touch the grass on the bank surrounding a field while she talked, in the way you might stroke the hair of a child or a beloved spouse, or in the glance at a field as she passed. One of the women described to me how, when she was young, she hated and resented having to work in the fields but how now she had learned to love it.

I frequently heard the villagers express grief at the sight of an abandoned rice field, as though their own bodies carried the pain and loneliness of the field's neglect. Rice fields are inherited and worked, very often for centuries by one family, so that the cessation of a field's cultivation means a rupture in a tradition of continuity of work and generation, as though a limb of the cultural body had died. Many of the farmers' graves are located beside or between the fields they cultivated in life—their bones planted with the rice in death.

Slowly, many of the fields around villages like Sora are becoming overgrown with weeds, their drainage ditches clogged, and the banks around the fields all but disappeared. As the fields die, so they become a visual barometer of the demise of the villages and of a way of life—the severing of a living link between the villagers themselves, future generations, their ancestors, and their gods, as they pass by on their way to and from their toil.

The rice grown in Sora was the best I had ever tasted, as was the local saké brewed from that rice. And in the cultivation of their own personal rice fields and vegetable gardens, they never made use of either chemical insecticides or artificial fertilizers. For fertilizer they simply used the contents of their cesspits and the rice husks as a mulch. The only place they used chemical fertilizers and insecticides was on the rice and tobacco grown for the government, in accordance with that government's directives. And even though the harvest of our final summer in Sora was ruined by a disastrous drought, we never needed to buy rice for the whole of the following winter, due to the selfless generosity of our neighbors.

In their gratitude for rice and their close identification with its propagation, the old people, particularly the women, seemed to feel a duty to continue the cultivation of their own family fields, long after the remaining members of the family had died or moved away and there was no longer any practical need. They would be the last in their family line to do so, even though they were so stricken by age and a lifetime's labor that they could only literally crawl around their fields on their hands and knees, going to and from them with the support of their prams. It was this extraordinary spiritual energy that enabled many of the women we knew to transcend serious illness and continue an active life.

The village is divided into groups of five households. These households share the work and responsibility for the upkeep and care of their particular part of the village, as well as sharing work at times of planting and harvesting both rice and tobacco. After the war, however, because of the difficulties in maintaining what had always been a self-sufficient agrarian economy, it was customary for the active members of families to leave the village and work in the cities on building sites and road construction in order to supplement incomes derived from their fields and fishing and support elderly parents or parents-in-law. Fortunately, nowadays several small, light industries have been introduced into the village in order to prevent the necessity for leaving. These vary from hand-weaving silk for kimono, which are made up in Kyoto, to small electric-loom shops, rice-straw rope making, and the machine production of curtains.

The women weavers of kimono material weave when the weather is bad and farm when the weather is fine, their hands moving naturally from the fields to the shuttle and loom and back again. In winter when the fields are at rest, they marry warp and weft as skillfully for a kimono to be worn at a spring tea ceremony as they plant out rice in the spring in patterns across the sky-reflecting fields around the village—rice that will fill bowls in the depths of winter.

> I *love these old women,*
> *whose skin resembles*
> *the earth they till,*

and whose backs are bent
horizontal
from bowing to it
so long.
They laugh so easily,
these earthwomen,
and show the gold
that fills their mouths.

PART TWO

◆ Village Japan ◆

Map of Sora Village

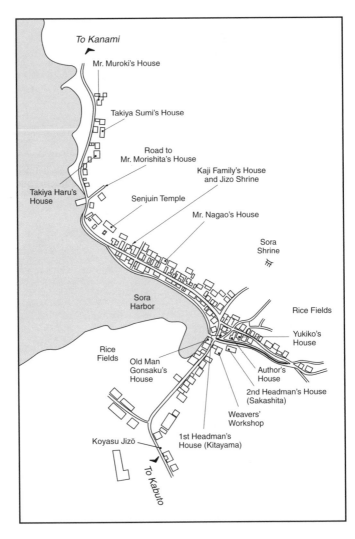

To Kanami

Mr. Muroki's House

Takiya Sumi's House

Road to
Mr. Morishita's House

Kaji Family's House
and Jizo Shrine

Takiya Haru's
House

Senjuin Temple

Mr. Nagao's House

Sora
Shrine

Sora
Harbor

Rice Fields

Yukiko's
House

Rice
Fields

Old Man
Gonsaku's
House

Author's
House

2nd Headman's House
(Sakashita)

Weavers'
Workshop

Koyasu Jizō

1st Headman's
House (Kitayama)

To Kabuto

◆ Village Children

At half past three each day, the afternoon silence of the village would evaporate as the bright voices of children returning home slowly increased in volume the nearer they approached the village down the hill from the school. Their voices filled the village lanes like noisy flocks of birds alighting in the branches of a tree. They carried a transformative energy with them—samurai battles, Martian expeditions, circuses of wild beasts, the strange walks and body postures of internal theater—a troupe of diminutive players and shape-shifters from the shamanic primary school over the hill, terrorizing the village cats and mesmerizing the dogs. Usually, behind the main cast of these impromptu performances came, straggling solitarily, a girl of about seven years of age who was mentally disabled in some way, locked in sometimes earnest, sometimes excited conversations with herself or some spectral companion. We never discovered the nature of her condition.

On spring and summer afternoons, the children would disperse to their various homes, only to reappear mounted on bicycles, circumnavigating the village in Formula One races or orbiting space stations, or to amble silenced and trancelike from the village shop, their worlds suddenly centripetal and constellated around the taste-aura of an ice cream or candy bar.

On summer evenings after dark, the street-lit arena of the vermilion bridge would become the focus of small, excitedly chattering crouched bodies collecting *kabuto-mushi* (the Atlas beetle, which is shaped like a samurai helmet and known in Japan as the "helmet beetle"), prized pets among village children, as they were felled from the night air by the seductive and illusory sun of the street lamp, which was always shaded by a frenetic galaxy of bugs and moths.

Sadly, the evidence of such nocturnal hunts would sometimes be only too obvious the following morning, with a litter of insect armory scattered across the road like the aftermath of a medieval battle observed from the air.

◆ Summer Nights

On summer nights it was often too hot to remain in the house, and there was a need to seek out the water's edge. The best way was to walk through the village main street to the space in front of the temple. There the air was cool, where it had been steeping over the water.

The street was unlit, except for a lamp over the vermilion bridge and another near the front of the temple at the other end of the village. Apart from these, there were only the dim lights in the houses, lights that strayed only a few feet from their source and offered no illumination to the street.

This darkness, with the lack of visual distraction, however, became the bed on which a multilayered soup of olfactory and aural delights was laid down—a place for sensory-sipping at the village's most intimate and interior life. As you passed down the street, at every few breath-steps a particular stratum of this blend would separate and predominate briefly before fusing back into the environmental mix. The smells of incense, feces, cooking, kerosene, urine, cedar-wood smoke, seawater, freshly sawn pine, fish, diesel oil, warm clay walls, and old rope. These scents, subtle and mysterious, familiar and alien, coarse and refined, stench and perfume, were accompanied by an evening raga of sounds—household altar-bells and evening sutra chanting, shrill-echoing bathroom voices of children, sliding *karakami*, television, the slap of water on hulls as a passageway to the quay was passed, rhythmic chopping from a kitchen window, complaining cats, and the distant roar of a boat opening its throttle to the dark bay beyond.

It was these smells and sounds, more than the visual environment, that transmitted the unfamiliar and seemingly secret life of the village that first year and created an impression of mystery and strangeness. Yet paradoxically, at the same time there was present a recognition and resonance—in some very deep place an almost forgotten familiarity—like recognizing, at a culturally and historically undifferentiated, collective level, a rhythm-texture of life that combines the mundane-domestic with something ancient and sacred, which still lingers on the horizon of recall.

> In the night,
> the voice
> of an unknown bird,
> passes
> from one dream
> to another.

◆ "Second Home" Villages

Between the villages of Sora and Kabuto, on a curve in the coast that rounds out from the east end of Sora and into the little bay of Zenzuka to the Sora side of Helmet Mountain, there is an abandoned hamlet of some twelve or so houses. They are holiday or weekend homes and vary in design from pseudo-backwoods cabins to much more substantial constructions complete with gardens and small outhouses. This holiday hamlet was established at the time of Japan's "bubble economy" when there was a plan to build a bridge from this part of the peninsula across to Noto Island. Someone with an eye to rapid yen bought the land, cleared it, and divided it into building plots, which they sold to city dwellers who, along with their new acquisition of wealth, were also buying the idea of a "second home"—a fairly new but increasingly popular concept in Japan.

Eventually the site of the planned bridge was moved some fifty miles down the coast, and the "bubble," having risen to insupportable heights, burst as bubbles must, leaving houses that had only been used for a season or two empty and the promise of as-yet-unconnected electricity broken along with the bubble.

The hamlet is left deserted, but as though families might have been going to return after an outing, since many of the houses are still equipped with the basic domestic necessities. They remain waiting, with the slow onset of decay setting in on wooden porches, etching through the thin metal of domestic kerosene tanks attached to the outside walls of bathrooms, and discoloring the pods of gas bottles below kitchen windows. Now, bamboo and wild camellias push up against walls and doors and trail across roofs, slowly reclaiming the site for the forest, while spiders stand sentinel at the center of their mandalas, across gateways and porches, or move in and furnish silent rooms with soft drapes.

It is like a hamlet that has fallen victim to ethnic cleansing or rampant plague. There is a melancholy along this shore below the houses on summer evenings, of broken dreams. But by autumn, the low afternoon light translates this into another language—the bitter images of dereliction and thwarted greed.

As I walked along the potholed road by the shore past these empty dwellings, I could not help thinking of the "cardboard cities" of the homeless within the cities of Britain and now Tokyo, too, in these days of recession. The waste of money, workmanship, and materials not to mention land, once wild and beautiful, disturbed to no purpose contrasting achingly with the rice fields around Sora, shaped by devotion, while at the same time shaping that devotion, for generations; a land whose elemental energies are still honored, but a land that is fast-changing.

At the end of the hamlet where the road dwindles and fades out into wilderness, there is a track that leads past an abandoned clubhouse down to the shore, where two huge stone images of Daikoku and Ebisu (gods of rice farming and fishing, respectively) stand on either side of a thin path that ends on a tiny, rocky promontory. On the promontory stands a single, small wind-bent pine, and at its foot there is a small Shintō shrine dedicated to the tutelary deity of sailors, Konpira. Ironically, and symptomatic of the changing tide of consciousness, the area around this shrine is littered with the debris of picnic meals and discarded equipment left by weekend fishermen. An area once considered sacred is now ignored and polluted—Daikoku and Ebisu, increasingly strangers in their own land.

Some miles to the other side of Sora between the villages of Kanami and Iwaguruma there is another larger settlement of "second homes." This one and the one at Zenzuka, though, present a stark contrast. Here, one emerges from the rough single-track road past rice fields and areas of scrub onto, or rather into, something that makes you feel you suddenly changed discs in a virtual reality visor or crossed an environmental/time Rubicon between two realities. You cruise into a world of macadamized and discretely lamped suburban politeness, between brown raised brows of shaved and dehydrated lawns fronting wooden kit houses that seem to have been birthed from between the sheets of a catalogue of the American Dream. This is a "second home" village with clout and image and gardens, where anything natural is crucified and a sofa and two armchairs would not look out of place on the lawn. It is situated just above and beyond a small marina, ironically called Tsubaki-ga-saki ("Camellia Headland"), since the camellias were served eviction notices, and where they have survived (perhaps brought in from a garden center) have been forced to conform with the plastic garden-furniture.

From this instant village to its adjacent marina with antiseptic gleams from hulls of fiberglass and alloy craft, resembling an uneasy hybrid of high-tech jewelry and kitchen gadgetry, all express a bleakness of spirit and make you feel you have somehow been teleported into a television commercial. It is a sudden impact of culture shock and lasts for three to five minutes, depending on the speed with which you pass through.

◆ Noto Roads

For the first few months after our arrival in Sora, we decided that we were going to walk wherever the distance was walkable (for example, to the railway station in the next village) and hire a taxi for any longer journeys. After a few months, however, we bought bicycles to try and save some money on taxi fares. Finally, after nearly a year, because of our precarious financial state and a request for me to hold English classes in the nearest town, Anamizu, we succumbed to buying a very cheap second-hand car.

The car was white and shaped like a shoe. Not only was it shaped like a shoe but it was about the size of a large shoe. It was almost necessary for me to shoehorn myself into it, and for the first few days I was convinced I would never be able to drive it, as my thighs were jammed up against the steering wheel! Slowly, over a period of weeks some kind of fusion occurred between my body length and the tiny car's interior, and we—car and I—drove. I felt like a cyborg.

Driving to and from my English class in Anamizu

throughout the year, the roads and lanes provided a kind of seasonal calendar with the creatures that frequented their surfaces and made driving a hazardous business, not least of course for them. Winter was a fairly void period, except for the obvious dangers of snow, ice, and the occasional cat. Spring, however, sprung in with frogs. Tiny, green plastic-contents-of-a-Christmas-cracker-looking frogs, which leapt about all over the road like extras in an Old Testament epic. Frogs that played chicken as they crossed the road, causing you to swerve from one side to the other and appear around corners to oncoming tractors, on the wrong side.

On the disappearance of these kamikaze leapers, they were replaced by huge bloated bullfrogs, that while not frenetically suicidal were as static as bollards in their waiting game with karma. These amphibians were natural meditators and in no way disturbed by the approach of a motor vehicle.

As soon as the temperature rose and evenings lengthened, this became the cue for queues of snakes, some huge six-foot serpents, to lie like hoses or temporary traffic-light cables across the road, bringing your forehead sharply up against the warm glass of the windscreen as you jammed your foot down on the brake to make detours, gingerly at 3 kph, as though you feared your tires might get bitten. Most often, you sadly passed the poor creatures already gutted, dissected; their heads bruised by nothing more transcendental than a Bridgestone tire.

The snakes remained until early autumn, and although the car was furnished with the obligatory talisman from a Buddhist temple and a charm from a Shintō shrine, prayer was still a necessary adjunct. But no sooner was it on your lips than "it" appeared. Manifested in thousands of small praying forms on the asphalt before you were praying mantises, hunched like little monks on an autumnal pilgrimage.

◆ Helmet Mountain (Kabuto Yama)

Shortly after our arrival in Sora we walked to Helmet Mountain, a forested hill that juts out into the sea. It is shaped like a samurai helmet, hence its name, and is situated about equidistantly, two miles either way, between the villages of Sora and Kabuto, a village named after the hill. At the top of Helmet Mountain there is a Shintō shrine, the object of our visit.

The shrine is reached by a long flight of weathered and eroded steps, which stretch from the granite *torii* (shrine gateway) at the bottom of the hill to the shrine at the top. Just before you arrive at the top, there is a kind of landing or break in the flight of steps intersected by paths leading to the left and to the right. These are in fact one and the same path which forms a circle just beneath the summit of the hill where the shrine is located. I assumed that this path must have been used in some of the Shintō ceremonies, for circumambulating the shrine in a clockwise (sunwise) direction, and on a later inquiry found this to be so.

The shrine, typical of those in the area, consists of two attached buildings, one behind the other, with the larger one in front, the smaller (the inner sanctum) behind. The front part of the shrine contains the usual paraphernalia, including a large drum, the *mikoshi* (an elaborate palanquin-like portable shrine in which the kami, or something representing the kami, is temporarily housed while it is carried through the district over which it presides) mounted on two trestles, and a box for donations. In front of the donation box hangs a red-and-white rope at the top of which is a slit bell, like a large cow bell, which emits a dull metallic rattling sound when shaken by the rope in order to attract the attention of the kami and to concentrate and calm the mind of the worshiper before he or she prays to the kami. Above the donation box hangs a board on which are painted the names of the war dead, and to the left, a model of a fishing boat, presumably left there by the owner of the vessel for protection. Or perhaps by families of the fishermen who have already perished with the boat.

Beyond the donation box suspended between two pillars is a rope made of rice straw with strips of white paper cut in zigzags hanging from it at intervals. Called a *shimenawa*, it indicates that the area beyond the rope is the sacred dwelling place of the kami. At the back of this space and directly in front of the entrance to the inner sanctum, there is a large mounted mirror of polished metal, symbolizing both the numinous and pure nature of the kami as well as the fidelity of the worshiper. On either side of the mirror are ancient wooden images of two former priests.

The energy at the top of Helmet Mountain is very powerful, and it always affected my body in some way or other, at certain times more powerfully than at others. We were told by a local farmer that it had once been a nesting place of eagles. It was a place I would return to quite regularly.

A shrine like this has no resident priest living within its compound. It is only visited at certain festival or ceremonial occasions. The rest of the year it is a silent and solitary place, except for the occasional visit by a local on some personal business.

As we descended the hillside and walked through the forest, we came across a clearing where someone had made a vegetable garden. While admiring the neatly weeded rows of winter vegetables, a very ancient-looking woman who might have stepped out of a folktale emerged from the forest to one side of the garden. On seeing us, she broke into a smile and we all bowed "Konnichiwa." "Where are you from?" she asked, looking from Masako to me, and obviously surprised to see a foreigner.

"We've just moved into Sora. Into Mr. Sawada's house beside the vermilion bridge," answered Masako. "My husband is from Britain and I'm from Tokyo. But we've decided to live in the Japanese countryside."

"Ah, good. Mr. Sawada's house. Yes, I know," she said smiling. "You've come to a good place. The land here is very soft and gentle, like the people. We never have earthquakes here. In all my years I never remember there being an earthquake."

Three nights later, I had just gone upstairs and begun to undress when, as I put out my hand to hang my shirt on a large *ikō* (a lacquered stand for hanging kimono), it appeared to move away from me. At the same time, my body registered that certain feeling of instability that had become familiar while I was living in Tokyo. But I did not, in those few seconds, make the connection, after the reassurance we had received from the old woman on Helmet Mountain, until I realized that not only the *ikō* but the room, in fact, the whole house was moving—we were having an earthquake!

We hurried to the radio and waited for any reports, and learned that the epicenter had apparently been deep under the sea near the town of Wajima on the other side of the peninsula. There had been some damage to the harbor, and a car had fallen into the sea, but there had been no injuries or loss of life.

I hoped that the locals would not associate the appearance of a foreigner in their midst with the earthquake, as some form of retribution devised by the local kami.

◆ An Offer I Could Not Refuse

While trying to acquaint ourselves with the topography of the area, we were walking through the village one afternoon when something made me turn and glance over my shoulder. I just caught sight of the back of a priest in yellow-and-white robes disappearing around the corner of a house. The experience for some reason gave me a powerful feeling of *déjà vu* that registered in my body physically, like a shock. I had expected to see the black robes of a priest of the Jōdo Shin sect of Pure Land Buddhism in the village, but this brief flash was far more exotic. Without thinking of any other Japanese sect, I had for some reason immediately associated the image with Tibetan monks, some of whose robes share similar colors of yellow and white. Nevertheless, when I thought about it I realized that this association possibly made sense, if in fact the temple in the village belonged to the Shingon sect, since there are many shared features between the two forms of Buddhism; hence, my association at some subliminal level, perhaps.

We had already decided that we should call on the temple, and I was now curious to see if my hunch was correct. A few days later we paid a visit, bearing the customary gifts, only to find that the priest was out, but to be invited back later by the priest's wife, who told us that the temple did indeed belong to the Shingon sect. A day or two later, the priest, Reverend Tani, phoned and invited us to dinner the following evening.

When we arrived at the temple, we were shown into a room at the back of Reverend Tani's house, where he served us green tea while we sat around a *hibachi* (a traditional form of heating). Almost his first words were: "How long do you think you will stay in this village?"

I answered him honestly, that I never tried to plan too much ahead in my life but rather preferred to wait and see which direction it tended toward. After a few more minutes of general conversation he suddenly asked: "Do you think you can live in this village?"

My reply, in the affirmative, seemed to please him, because he extended an arm across the *hibachi* and warmly shook my hand with a broad smile on his face. Then Mrs. Tani silently slid open the *karakami* and announced that dinner was ready.

We were shown into a large, long room with three low, lacquered tables placed end to end and covered in dishes containing various kinds of vegetables, shellfish, meats, and fish. Already sitting at the tables were Mrs. Tani's uncle and aunt, Mr. and Mrs. Shinde, who live in the fishing port town of Ushitsu some thirty kilometers up the coast from Sora, and her father, Reverend Terakoshi, also a Shingon priest.

We introduced ourselves in the traditional, formal Japanese manner, kneeling on the tatami and bowing deeply to each other. It was explained that Mr. Shinde worked in a senior post on the Ushitsu District Council and had played a key role in preserving and promoting interest in a large Jōmon period (Neolithic) site close to where he had also been in charge of the founding of a hot-spring spa (*onsen*), to which we were later to become frequent visitors. Reverend Terakoshi had a large and beautiful temple in a nearby town.

Seated on cushions (*zabuton*) at the table, we first toasted each other with chilled Japanese beer before commencing the feast that was set before us. I had hardly lifted my bowl of miso soup, however, when Reverend Tani turned to me and said: "I want you to come and look after this temple and live in it rent free. We have to go to another temple in Nakai. Do you think you can do that?"

We had been in the temple little more than half an hour, and already we were being asked if we would take care of it. I was so taken aback that without any space to think about it I immediately agreed, saying we would be very pleased to do so. Later, Reverend Tani told us he too was taken completely by surprise, as he had had no idea of making such a request. To add to the strangeness of the circumstances of the offer, Reverend Tani, at the time, had no idea that I had been a Buddhist for nearly twenty years, albeit of a different school from the Shingon sect.

Or that I had on two previous occasions in my life, been on the point of taking ordination as a Buddhist priest.

Only one thing concerned me, and that was how the people of such a small conservative village would accept the idea of a foreigner moving into their temple. This had obviously occurred to Reverend Tani also, because a few days later he asked us not to mention it to anyone until he had had a meeting with the temple elders, since the unexpectedness of his asking us had preempted any plans that would need to be made.

Some weeks later, we had gone for a walk through the village at night, when suddenly there were voices up ahead of us in the dark, coming from the temple end of the village. Against the only street lamp at that end of the village, the silhouettes of a group of people could be seen coming toward us. As they drew close and we greeted one another, they recognized us and one of the men detached himself from the group, while the others carried on down the street.

Approaching us in the dark, the man bowed and said to Masako, "We are delighted that you are going to take care of the temple and we would like it if your husband would use one of the rooms over the temple to work in. But I'm sorry, we do find it a bit difficult to think of anyone but a priest living there because all our ancestors are there."

We explained that we understood their feelings completely and thanked them for their generosity in allowing me to work there, while promising to do our best in looking after the temple.

As we continued our walk, it dawned on us that they must have just come from a meeting with Reverend Tani, and we hoped they would not think that we were already on our way to the temple on some prearrangement with him to be informed of the outcome of the meeting.

By the end of the year, the barrier to our living in the

temple had dissolved, but by that time I had found that cycling or walking to and from the temple each day, and dividing the hours between working at my desk and working in the temple and its garden, a very agreeable rhythm.

All spring and summer long and well into the autumn, I worked upstairs in the temple, and during breaks, cleaned the *hondō* (the main hall containing the image of the Buddha or Buddhist deity to which the temple is dedicated) and weeded the garden. In the winter, however, it became too cold to remain in the temple without heating of some kind, and I took to working at home and visiting the temple daily just to burn incense and make a daily check, particularly if there had been bad weather, or to make things secure if a typhoon had been forecast.

On arriving at the temple at any time of the year, I often found small offerings left either inside the *hondō* before the main altar or outside in front of the images of Jizō, Kannon, or Fudō-myōō. These offerings ranged from rice left at the main altar in brilliantly colored silk bags made from the remnants of old kimono to small balls of rice, wildflowers and grasses, hundred-yen pieces, candles and incense placed where someone had prayed on their way to their fields in the early morning.

From my workroom window at the temple, overlooking the road and the sea, I often saw that the old people still retained the custom of bowing to the temple as they passed by either on foot, bicycle, or tractor.

Not being involved in farming or fishing, but remaining in the village and working at my table while everyone else worked in the surrounding fields or at sea, at first made me wish for a boat or a field. But I soon realized that making ourselves available for driving our neighbors from one place to another and caretaking the temple meant that we could at least offer something to the community, which helped make us feel a little more integrated.

The sun's dying
slowly
dims the village,
but the cackle of
an old crone
suddenly
gifts the dusk
with gold!

◆ Ao-Daishō (Great Blue Snake)

One spring morning when I was still working at home, I was sitting at my worktable when for some reason I turned my head to the left toward the window on that side of the room. There, pressed up against the glass, was the head of a huge snake. I got up from the table and went over to look at it. It seemed to be staring straight into my eyes. I spoke to it for a while, more in the way of expressing surprise to myself and wondering aloud what it might be wanting. Then, slowly sliding the window open, I found that its body extended the length of the wall to the right of the window and then out of sight somewhere around the side of the house. The snake was quite obviously over six feet in length, with a strange green-bluish hue, reminding me that this was a snake someone had described to us. It is called *ao-daishō*, or "great blue snake," is harmless and seen as auspicious—it is a guardian snake. Snakes are often understood as messengers of a kami or indeed a manifestation of the kami itself.

Ao-daishō remained staring into the room for fifteen minutes or more without moving a scale. Then it slowly moved back down the windowpane and entered the house through a hole in the weatherboarding just beneath the sill and into the space between my workroom floor and the room below containing the Buddhist altar.

From this time on, the house, which had been overrun by a plague of mice, became entirely mouse-free.

Often, in the early hours before the village had woken, I would hear a sound in the house that was different from the sparrows stirring under the eaves or the contact-sound of the feet of a heron or kite on the roof. It was the sound of footless walking—*ao-daishō* moving through the interior of the house on a dawn glide.

◆ Koyasu Jizō (Bodhisattva that protects women in childbirth)

I had been examining a stone which was standing to one side of the *torii* gate at the foot of Helmet Mountain one afternoon and noticed that carved on the stone was a Sanskrit character, known in esoteric Buddhism as a "seed syllable" (*bija*), enthroned on a lotus blossom. It suggested that the Shintō shrine on Helmet Mountain had once been associated with a Shingon temple in the area, most likely Senjuin, the temple in Sora. As we were walking away from the stone, Old Man Gonsaku suddenly emerged from some bushes beside the path ahead of us with a sheaf of leaves in his hand. When he saw us approaching, he explained that he had been picking small branches of the *sakaki* tree, which is sacred to Shintō, to offer to the kami of his household shrine.

We walked with him to where he had left his bicycle and watched him as he stripped some unwanted leaves from the twigs and placed them in a basket mounted on the front. Then the three of us walked back toward the village, Old Man Gonsaku pushing his bicycle, which was almost as tall as he was. As we walked, he talked (punctuated with giggling which we came to learn was a feature of and accompaniment to any conversation with Old Man Gonsaku), of how once Eikoku (Great Britain) and Japan had been enemies. And how Eikoku had won and we were now friends. He said that now the West was above Japan, describing it in terms of the feudal image of a pyramidal hierarchy. He told us how the priest at the shrine used to exhort them to pray for victory in the war against America and its allies.

As we entered the village, we passed by an old image of the Buddhist bodhisattva Jizō enshrined by the roadside. I asked him if he knew anything about this particular image's history. He said that he did, and that it was a very interesting story. I asked him if he would mind coming to our house to tell us about it, and we made an arrangement for tea time the following day.

By half-past four the next day, Old Man Gonsaku had not appeared. Looking toward his house, I could see no sign of movement, so assumed he must either have been sleeping or gone out and forgotten. Having not walked that day, I decided to go out, saying to Masako, "I bet you, as soon as I open the door he'll arrive." I put my notebook into a small hessian bag and, slinging it over my shoulder, I slipped into my shoes in the *genkan*. Sure enough, as I slid back the front door, there was Old Man Gonsaku emerging from his own house. He spotted me and called, "Oh, you're going out."

"No," I shouted back. And beckoned, "Come in, we're waiting for you."

It was the first time Old Man Gonsaku had been in our house. He entered the *genkan* shyly, removing his cap and carrying it in one hand with a lime-green hand towel in the other. I showed him into the large room that contained the household altar and offered him a cushion in the place of honor in front of the *tokonoma*. At first he refused it, but after a little persuasion, he finally settled down onto it, placing his blue, peaked cap beside him on the tatami and his green towel in his lap.

Masako came into the room with a tray of small cups and glasses and a bottle of saké. A broad smile spread across his face and he giggled as he turned the bottle around so that he could read the label: Sōgen (a good local saké in Far Noto). Although we normally prefer to heat it, the weather was already very hot and humid so we decided to drink it cold.

Old Man Gonsaku was unshaven as usual, having a bristly mustache and bearded chin, while the rest of his face was naturally hairless. His head hair was abundant and very coarse, so that it stuck up like a brush. His ears were huge with long broad lobes, like the ears on the images of Buddhas and bodhisattvas. The upper lids of his eyes had relaxed with age and all but obscured his vision so that in order to see ahead he had to tilt his head back slightly. As was also usual, his fly was open.

I passed him the tray of cups and glasses and he chose a medium-sized cup. Masako and I both chose a glass each. I poured out the saké and the three of us toasted, "Kanpai!" I then turned on the tape recorder, after asking him if he objected to it, and reminded him that he was going to tell us the story of the Jizō image we had passed the previous day.

Old Man Gonsaku's face was glistening with sweat and he scrubbed it with his green towel. Then laying the towel to one side, he began to rub his knees with the palms of each hand in a circular motion, as though trying to raise the energy of the story up from his legs that had walked him into the situation of telling it in the first place. As he spoke he frequently broke off in giggles which seemed to percolate from the extremities of his body and converge in his chest, so that their collective momentum caused his body to bob up and down as his throat acted as their escape valve. "A long, long time ago, we had no doctors and no midwives in this village. Only the old women of the village. By the way, we call the midwife *toriage babā*, a woman who takes a baby out of its mother's body. In those days, it was a very serious and worrying business for women, you know, if their babies had difficulty getting out of their bodies.

"In this village, when a woman gives birth her husband's not allowed in the room. Not even any of her boy children should be there. It's all women's business. Not men's. I was told that if I broke that custom, I would have been punished. I don't know what sort of punishment I would have had," he giggled. "Anyway, only women could attend, to help in the birth.

"The village people began to think they needed some kind of protection for women in childbirth. Eventually, they decided to have Jizō-sama [*sama* is an honorific], and one of the village people carved a Jizō-sama out of stone." Then he added, scratching his belly, "I don't know where the stone came from." He picked up his cup and, looking lovingly into it, took a sip.

"People knew that spirit should be put into Jizō-sama, you know, otherwise it would only be a piece of stone. It is the same as putting spirit into a carved *hotoke-sama* [*hotoke* is colloquial for Buddha]. But none of the village people knew how to do it.

"Now we have a temple here, and you know the temple people very well. But a long time ago there was no monk here. There might have been someone like an unqualified monk, but he didn't know how to put spirit into Jizō-sama. So the people decided to wait for a traveling monk to visit the temple. You know, in those days lots of monks traveled from village to village chanting and begging.

"One day at last a monk arrived, and one of the men asked him, 'Aren't you Ikkyū-sama?' And the monk replied, 'Yes.' I don't know whether he was a Zen monk or a Shingon monk, but I was told his name was Ikkyū. Anyway, people asked Ikkyū-sama to put a spirit into Jizō-sama, and they were very curious to know how he would do it." He took a careful sip of saké and then started a giggling fit. "So they gathered round and watched Ikkyū-sama with great interest. Do you know what he did?" He was bobbing up and down and giggling uncontrollably. "Ikkyū-sama tucked up his robe and he pissed all over Jizō-sama's head!"

It took a time for our collective laughter to subside, and I realized at this point that he had for the last few minutes been intermittently touching his genitals, as if contacting the source of the story's charge or completely identifying with the narrative. "Then Ikkyū-sama said, 'Well, this Jizō's now got a spirit so it is all-powerful. If you believe in this Jizō, women in the village can deliver their babies safely.' Then he left."

He was giggling again. "The villagers looked at each other. They were a bit upset. 'How disgusting! How filthy!' they said to each other. And they decided that this Jizō-sama should be cleaned, so they carried it down to the river and scrubbed it.

"That night, Jizō-sama appeared in the house of one of the men who had washed it and said, 'Why did you wash me? I want to be pissed on again, otherwise I can't be Koyasu Jizō. And don't wash me again!' Then Jizō-sama disappeared. I think it was a kind of revelation he had in a dream."

I refilled his cup and our glasses, and he mopped his face very thoroughly with his towel as I asked him why he thought Jizō needed to be pissed over in order to put spirit into him. He was silent and looked up at the ceiling and then down at the table. He took in a breath and let it out and stared off into a horizonless perspective. "I've been wondering why Jizō-sama needed to be pissed on over his head. You know, I think the reason is this. A baby comes out around this area." He was pointing toward his still-open fly, and I was wondering if it was actually pissing that was involved here and not something else. "I heard this story from old people when I was small. I might be the only person who knows this story, that's why I can tell it to you. Was it interesting?" We assured him that it was very interesting. "Do you think I'm a funny old man? A long, long time ago old people told me this story," he repeated, as though trying to emphasize a genuine provenance for it. "These days we have a clinic in Kabuto and a hospital in Anamizu, but still people are looking after Jizō-sama."

As I refilled his cup again, I thought how this story must have attracted him since he was such a great public pisser himself. He replaced his cup on the table after it was filled and told us how he was only allowed to drink two cups a day, but they were big cups, and the cup he was presently drinking from was small by comparison. This was followed by more giggles, before he continued, "The other Jizō-sama near the school is not old. It was put there in my parents' day. When I was young, the road up the hill to Kabuto was very narrow and lonely, so a village man donated the Jizō-sama to guard people traveling along it. He died about thirty years ago."

There had once been a very strong shamanistic tradition, particularly amongst the women in these country areas, and I was curious about his memories of any local healers. He thought for a moment. "Old Woman Yoshioka, who lived two doors away from my house, used to heal people. But when doctors arrived in the area, people gradually stopped visiting her.

"I also knew a man and a woman in Ukawa [a nearby village] who healed people. They could even talk with your dead relations for you. The man made people sit and pray in front of a folding gold screen, which was supposed to produce healing energy. I heard that one very rich man bought the screen and slept in front of it every night, but that he was never healed and just got worse. In the end, he became skin and bone. By the time his family took him to a doctor it was too late. The healer was reported to the police, but he earned lots of money with his swindles.

"I think there used to be healers in all the villages. I knew a man who destroyed a Buddha image he had bought from someone who had told him that if he worshiped it his sick daughter would be healed. But his pretty daughter died. I knew an old woman in this village. Her house was near the farmer's cooperative. I don't know whether she could really heal or not."

Old Man Gonsaku sipped at his saké and, giggling, seemed to change raconteural gear. "I once worked as a boatman, shipping logs and charcoal and other things from this village, Kabuto, and Ukawa to Takaoka City on the other side of the bay. I was employed by a Toyama man."

He suddenly stopped and pointed at the tape recorder with a thick, hardworked forefinger that bore evidence of a lifetime's labor. "This small machine is recording what I am saying now?" I assured him that it was. I was constantly intrigued by many of the villager's amazement at and apparent ignorance of the sophisticated technologies their own country produced. "Yes," I told him , "You'll be able to listen to your voice later on."

He was giggling and holding his genitals again. "I used to be . . ." he hesitated and looked from me to Masako and then back again to me. "I used to be a bit of a waster, indeed. I spent all my money on, you know, sixteen is very young, and all my fellow boatmen were older than me. They took me to a brothel. I was probably only fifteen at the time. They all clapped, saying that I had become a man. Of course, it was before I got married. Anyway, I wasted all my money. So in the end my employer and my parents made an agreement that I wasn't to be paid directly. It was to go to them first."

From time to time he picked up his cap and looked inside it. I thought at first that this action meant he was preparing to go home but soon came to realize that it was like a ritual for recollection or concentration—almost as though the circle of the cap kept him within the sphere of the particular arena of memories he was recounting.

He was silent for a while and raised his head to look up at the ceiling. Suddenly he was bouncing up and down again and giggling. "My *taiko* drumming is the same type as Wajima's (a town on the peninsula, famous for *taiko*). In Wajima four drummers play on one drum, but in this village two drummers play on one drum at festivals. One of the drummers died some years ago, so now I'm the only drummer here. I never learned from anyone how to play; I just watched and listened to others playing. You can see me drumming on the day of the festival. You must come.

"Sora is a very small village, but there used to be maybe five shrines altogether. But I think it was in Taishō 3 (1914) that all the shrines were made into one shrine— the present one. You know, Sora Shrine. The kami-sama in that shrine is the ancestor of the Hosoki family. You know, the house with the gate with the thatched roof. That's theirs. They were the oldest and richest family in the village. The present owner of that house is now living in Osaka.

"When we had five shrines it seemed everyday was a festival! People from other villages joked, 'You had a festival only yesterday, and again today?'" He put on a mask of amazement and we all laughed. "These days we only celebrate twice a year, April and September." He picked up his cup. "In those days the roads were very narrow so it was difficult to carry the portable shrine through the village. Sometimes we had to put it in a boat. These days it's easy but we don't have enough young men to carry the *mikoshi* on their shoulders."

He suddenly stood up. Whenever he stood up or sat down, it always took me by surprise. The effect was due to the shortness of his legs, causing his body to be already close to the ground. It was more as though the earth came up to meet him or fell away from him, similar to the way a baby is all of a sudden sitting or standing. "I must get back to my *babā* (old wife). She'll be wondering where I am."

I followed him to the *genkan* and watched him carefully negotiate the step and put on his shoes. He backed out through the doorway, bowing deeply and thanking us politely. We met his bows and thanked him also politely and very gratefully.

It is highly unlikely in the above story about the Koyasu Jizō, that the monk called Ikkyū was in fact the famous fourteenth-century Zen Master and poet of the same name, in spite of his eccentric and wild reputation. There is, however, an apocryphal story about him that, while expressing something of his own personality and the spirit of his Zen, does concern pissing.

Ikkyū was on a ferry where he met a fellow passenger who was a monk from one of the esoteric schools, most probably Shingon. The monk criticized Zen for ignoring magic, and in order to impress his captive audience he proceeded to invoke a tutelary deity called Fudō-Myōō (considered to be a manifestation of the Cosmic Sun Buddha Dainichi), who appeared in a halo of fire. Everyone was very frightened except Ikkyū, who calmly announced that he would match the monk's magic with his own. He would produce water from his body and extinguish the flames. So saying, he lifted his robes and pissed on the flames until Fudō-Myōō disappeared.

> The roof of a temple
> hangs in the dusk,
> like the wings
> of a great bird,
> hatching Buddhas.

◆ The Story of Zenzuka

In the summer and up until late autumn, we were in the

habit of swimming daily from the small beach in the little bay of Zenzuka, which was to the Sora side of Helmet Mountain surrounded by forest and small rice fields. We later learned from one of the women who worked in the fields around Zenzuka that they had been wondering all summer long what it was we did in the sea each day. They had come to the conclusion that we must have been diving for shellfish or something. Swimming for its own sake was not something that had entered their minds.

Sadly, the beach at Zenzuka collected a great deal of rubbish at times, thrown into the sea from villages down the coast and from over the sides of ships. A lot of the items washed up bore Korean *hangul* characters. It was sometimes necessary after a storm to clear up the beach before entering the water, which was always crystal clear and filled with an extraordinary variety of fish.

Zenzuka had always been a special place to me. Even the name "Zenzuka" carries an exotic and mysterious resonance like Zanzibar or Mandalay, and on hot summer days with a cool breeze off the sea, kites fishing in the bay, snakes sunbathing on the paths between the rice fields, and cicadas buzzing like mysterious energies coiling and uncoiling among the trees on the slopes of Helmet Mountain, it was like briefly being on a day visit to one of the heavenly realms. I was not at all surprised then to discover that there was a story about Zenzuka.

During the Kyōhō period (1716–36) there was a great famine in Noto that affected Sora very seriously. One day a boat carrying rice from Sakata in Yamagata prefecture was forced by a strong headwind to anchor in the tiny harbor of Sora to wait for a more favorable wind before continuing its voyage south. As soon as the starving villagers saw the boat, they thought a shipment of relief rice had reached them at last. Realizing their mistake, some of the villagers were forced to beg. On seeing their desperate plight and the pitiful condition of their skeletal bodies, and remembering how his master's warehouses were so filled with rice that even the mice were well-fed, the captain decided to unload at Sora.

That night the god Ebisu appeared beside the captain's pillow and told him to stop at Zenzuka on his way back to Sakata. But since they had already unloaded the rice there was no reason for them to continue their voyage. The next day, however, the weather was so beautiful they decided to set sail. As they were passing Zenzuka, a man appeared on the small rocky promontory (described in "Second Homes") and, waving with a fan, beckoned them into the tiny bay. As the boat came within earshot of the man, he shouted, "These rocks are precious, so load up with as many as you can."

The captain, thinking this to be a very strange order, was about to reconfirm what the man had said when the man disappeared. Then, remembering the words of Ebisu in his strange dream the previous night, and realizing that the man on the rocky promontory must have been Ebisu, he told his crew about it and ordered them to load the boat with rocks. By the time the boat had reached its home port of Sakata, the rocks in the boat had turned to gold.

The story of the completion of the voyage was carried back to Sora by the crews of other boats, and since that time a shrine has always been maintained on top of the small rocky promontory. In more recent times, giant statues of both Ebisu and Daikoku have stood guard at the entrance to the shrine.

◆ The Ideal Restaurant

While eating lunch in the Korean restaurant in Anamizu, the owner of which also ran the cesspit-emptying business, the person with whom I was lunching told me about a restaurant in Tokyo that a friend of his had told him about. While I suspect that the genesis of this story is probably to be found in an only-too-common enough experience in restaurants and has acquired a patination of fact through its entry into gastronomic folklore, it nevertheless carries an attractive idea. Apparently, this friend of his had gone into a restaurant, sat down, and after perusing the menu had ordered a meal from one of the waiters. When the meal was placed before him, he saw to his displeasure that it was not the meal he had asked for. He immediately complained to the waiter, who replied, "The policy of this restaurant is not to give people what they order."

This kind of restaurant is precisely what we need, I believe, as the perfect antidote to the hell of multichoice pampering that confuses us in so many areas of our consumer life. The idea that we should have everything we imagine we want rather than what we actually might need confines our lives even more blindly to the dictates of our narrowly conditioned egos, so limiting the possibilities of experiencing something we might be unprepared for or might otherwise wish to avoid—experiences that just might contain germs of new growth and knowledge. The nightmarish,extreme scenario in this respect is extended by the future prospect of genetic menus with "the baby of your choice," etc.—a world designed for those who can only live by the assurance of what is going to happen or of what conditions will be in the next second. A world of insurances and lawsuits against the unexpected, against life itself. In our optimism at finding such an establishment, however, we searched out this restaurant for ourselves on a trip to Tokyo, only to find that if it had existed, it had now vanished off the face of Japan.

◆ Mr. Nagao Speaks of Birth and Death

We met Mr. Nagao first at Sora Shrine on the occasion of the village spring festival. We had been told by Mr.

Kitayama, the headman, that Mr. Nagao came from a very old family that had occupied the same land for over 360 years and that he had been headman some few years previously and had lots of stories. When we met him, he was dressed formally in black *haori*, bearing his clan emblem, and *hakama* (kimono coat and men's silk culottes) in his capacity as the leader of the procession who purifies the path of the kami as it progresses through the village. He was short with a well-earthed body that gave a powerful impression of contained energy. He had a deep crease, probably a scar that ran around his jaw like a chinstrap and merged into the natural creases on either side of his face. He appeared to be in his mid-seventies.

It was January before we were able to arrange to visit him, when he had time after the busy harvest and preparations for winter to sit and talk. His study, where he kept records of the village and received visitors, was a small room on the west side of the house, decorated with his own ink paintings and calligraphy and with a view of the garden. At its center was an open hearth (*irori*), which instead of containing a wood fire had been cleared to provide space for a large kerosene stove. The room was stiflingly hot after the cold outside, and my spectacles steamed up immediately upon entering the room so that I had to remove them and wave them above the stove to warm the lenses. A television on the north wall of the room and opposite to where I was invited to sit was showing a panorama of mountain peaks. It was unaccountably left switched on for the duration of our visit, drawing my attention away periodically into different areas of Japan, the facial topography of politicians, the occasional flash of a war zone, and so on.

Mr. Nagao made green tea and passed cups to us while directing our attention to several small plates of rice crackers. After passing our cups, he leaned over to some shelves to his right and pulled out a document. Opening it and smoothing it with his hand, he said, "Before the Meiji period (1868–1912) we commoners weren't allowed to have surnames." He pointed, and I noticed that the first joint of each forefinger was bent toward its neighbor. "You can see my ancestor's name here, Satoemon [a given name]. This document shows how much rice families paid as tax. Our family status was based on the size of our crop, the number of mountains [for timber], and the amount of land we farmed. After the war even peasants could own land according to the land reforms, which meant that a period of equality had begun." As he talked, he would now and then point in one direction or another, indicating a temple, house, or field, raising his arm to stress some point he was making. Whenever he did this, what I imagined to be his elbow emitted a loud crack.

"The old family hierarchy is still reflected in the order of sitting in the temples. For example, in our temple, we have kept the old seating arrangements and you are required to donate a certain amount according to your status when the temple needs money for restoration or something like that. My temple is in Yamanaka, about twelve kilometers from here. At present my share is ¥150,000."

He folded the document and replaced it among the shelves, and we started to eat the rice crackers. The television showed the imperial crown princess walking up a flight of steps. She paused at the top to wave to somebody before disappearing into what appeared to be a black hole.

"Our lives have related deeply to rice from our earliest days," he said, spilling cracker crumbs from his mouth. "My mother gave birth to me on rice straw with the assistance of the old woman from next-door. A mother fed her newborn baby three times a day. She had to work in the rice and vegetable fields all day, so she fed her baby in the early morning before she left, at lunch time, and finally in the evening when she returned home. During the day I was put into a kind of round-shaped basket made of rice straw, with a rice-straw rope across each of my shoulders to stop me from climbing out. This is how I grew up.

"In my time, we only had four years of compulsory education. Beyond that it didn't matter whether you carried on or not. I remember that lots of my classmates brought their younger brothers or sisters to school on their backs and looked after them while they studied. I was lucky though. Because I was the family heir I received extra education, but none of my brothers and sisters did.

"In those days, Senjuin temple was always full of people, young and old, daytime and evening. Now it's no good, the young people are not there anymore. I feel closer to the temple than I do to the shrine. When you compare the shrine and the temple, not many Shintō priests live by the shrine but monks always live in a house attached to the temple."

An extraordinary commercial for diapers that showed a baby pissing from a cloud snatched my eyes and held them captive for a few seconds. He produced another old document from the shelves and prodded at it with the crooked joint of a forefinger, "This was written by my grandfather. . . Here he notes the religious gatherings . . . so many . . . January 5, 11, 12, . . . they gathered at the temple." He traced his finger along the characters, speaking each as the tip of his finger contacted it, as though it transmitted the vibration of the brushstrokes to his vocal chords. "Many activities. . . My grandfather recorded what they did and when, and so on. He writes that seven families belong to the Shin sect, Otani subsect; eight to the Shin sect, Nishi Honganji subsect; three to the Nichiren sect; eight to the Sōtō Zen sect, and fifty-eight to the Shingon sect. And concerning the shrine, he recorded. . . No, this is about funerals." He folded the document up again and spoke while sliding his palm up the crease of

the fold. "These days we burn the body at the town crematorium. But in the past we did it at the end of your
road, where the six Jizō are now. That's where we used to
burn the dead of the village.

"On the funeral eve, all the relations gathered and
spent all night together in front of the funerary altar. We
dressed the corpse in white with straw sandals on its feet
and a rosary in its hand. This is understood to be Kūkai's
[Kōbō Daishi] traveling outfit when he journeyed about
Japan. The corpse was put into the coffin sitting up, not
lying down like these days, and the coffin was shaped like
a tub and made of cedar. After the funeral, the body was
taken to that place at the end of your road to be burned
by the family and their relations. We laid a fire of twigs
and put the coffin on top. Then we covered it with rice
straw and then pine logs, till the coffin was completely
covered with rice straw and logs. We usually started to
burn the pyre at four o'clock in the afternoon, and it took
all night to completely burn the body." [Four is a number
associated with death in Japan because the pronunciation of its character is the same for that which means
"death".]

On the television, Buddhist monks were boarding a
plane. "While we were waiting, all the relations were invited back to the house for a meal, which was served on red-
lacquered, small, individual tray-tables (*akazen*). And we
ate rice mixed with red beans (*akameshi*). This is a tradition
we still keep. But every so often someone would go back
to check the state of the fire and see whether the corpse
was burning well or not." He laughed.

"A very natural funeral," I said, thinking that it was a
pity that we could not do the same today. "Speaking of
akazen, we found a large set of it in Mr. Sawada's barn.
Probably enough for twenty people or so. It's beautiful
Wajima lacquer."

"Did you? These days everything is changing. But we

still eat rice with red beans," he repeated. "The funerary altar was made by a local carpenter, and the ornaments were all arranged by the village people concerned. For example, we decorated it with artificial flowers made of paper. We made everything ourselves. But these days people are forgetting how to make things.

"My father died when I was nineteen, and I had to take part in all the village functions as head of my family, therefore I could learn a lot. We were born on rice straw and when we died, our bodies were covered with rice straw to be burned."

At that point, his youngest grandson, back from school, opened the *karakami* and stuck his head into the room, "Hello, Grandpa!"

> *When you were here,*
> *where were you?*
> *Now you are gone,*
> *where are you?*

◆ The Woman of 7,000 Steps

I first met Haru Takiya in the waiting room of the doctor's clinic in Kabuto Village where she was accompanied by her daughter and had come for a check-up. She was eighty-three and dressed in a smock over a traditional blue-and-white top and *monpe* (baggy work trousers). I noticed that she seemed very friendly and kept smiling and bowing forward on her seat, as though she wanted to say something. Her daughter explained that she had had to learn the British national anthem when she was a child at school, on the occasion of the visit of King George VI to Japan, and that she could still sing it word-perfect in English.

Haru Takiya leaned forward in her seat again and looked up at the sky through the clinic window. Then in a low, steady voice she began singing "God save our gracious King" till she reached the end, without faltering, and leaned back with a satisfied smile.

A week later, as we cycled through the village we came across Mrs. Takiya supporting herself on a buggy and passing by the steps that led up to the temple. When she saw us she stopped and bowed, and we dismounted from our bicycles beside her. She straightened up and then bent forward again, her large, worked hands, one resting on the other, on the handle of the buggy.

I asked her how she was, and she replied, "Not so bad. That day I met you in the clinic, the doctor told me I had to walk seven thousand steps a day," she laughed. "So I walk every day and count my steps. From my house to Tachibana's boat yard it's eighteen hundred steps there and back. To your house it's seventeen hundred steps one way. From my house to my daughter's it's fourteen hundred steps. And from my house to the shop it's one thousand steps.

"Where I walk depends on the weather. When I walk beside the sea I sing all the songs I learned at school. Then after singing all the ones I can remember, I sing the British national anthem twice. You know, I have to sing it twice, because it's a national anthem. No one can hear me, it's just for me."

A heron with its huge kimono sleeves almost dipping into the sea took off from a rock a little farther down from where we were standing on the road above the shore. It moved out, pacing its shadow across the inlet, toward a clump of reeds on the other side.

It was a warm day and we agreed how inviting the water looked. "I don't come from Sora," she said, still looking at the water. "I came to Sora from Ukawa. When I came to Sora, I discovered that none of the women swam in the sea. I had no swimming suit, so I swam in my underwear with my children.

"One day I noticed a man was swimming with me. The first woman to join me was Sumi Takiya, my next-door neighbor. I must have been the first woman in Sora to swim in the sea. That was more than sixty years ago.

"At that time, every autumn I used to come to Sora at dawn with an eight-sided candle-lantern to collect acorns in the temple compound here." She nodded toward the temple, with its huge, ancient *shii* tree [a kind of oak] in front of it. An almost imperceptible sigh rose from her body, like a piece of youthful breath that had been inhaled in that distant past beneath the branches of that great tree and retained in her body and was only now exhaled with the memory, as she looked up at the tree spreading against the sky. Then her eyelids dropped and she looked down at the road and agreed with herself that it had been a very long time ago.

"On sports day at the school, the parents were asked to run in a race, but I was the only woman who volunteered. The teacher told my children that they should be proud of their mother. 'We need more like her,' she said."

She had spoken of a time when she had been young and active, and perhaps by sharing the memories with us she had somehow in her own mind reaffirmed that reality, now that she was shackled by this counting to the back of a child's buggy.

Still leaning forward on her pram and laughing, she began to move off down the road. She had started counting again, her voice audible over her shoulder, as we remounted our bikes, sounding like a mantra or prayer directed to the realm she was already counting herself toward.

> Inevitably,
> *flesh shrinks back—*
> *bones wait their chance*
> *to shine.*

◆ Between Rivers

Living at the confluence of two rivers at our door meant our life was accompanied by the subtle back-rhythm of the waters' passage. This altered throughout the day and night and with the season, according to the state of the tide and the weather. As the tide turned, the waters of the sea and land met each other in a kind of "push hands" dance back and forth, till the sea either pushed farther into the land or the river into the sea, their waters mingling under the shadowy span of the vermilion bridge. Sometimes the water smelt of the sea; at other times, of earth and the breath of the forest.

Day and night the rivers on each side of the house and the stretch of water before the bridge where they met were attended by herons and the occasional kingfisher.

When all was still in the village, and particularly at night, you could hear the bill of a fishing heron as it tirelessly speared the water again and again in its desire to satisfy a nocturnal appetite. Now and then when it was standing vigil, strange creaking sounds were audible from somewhere in its long throat, as though it were thinking aloud to itself, or stood on a rusty spring in the river's bed.

I would often be awakened at night by a night-fishing heron, disturbed from its discipline and taking off in the dark with a purgatorial and Jurassic cry that seemed to stir in me some vestigial animal memory.

At other times, when the river was in full spate, or it was a spring tide, I would wake in the deep of the night with the waters sucking the underbelly of the bridge like waking to the sounds of lovemaking.

> *Where the river*
> *tells its stones,*
> *a heron appears,*
> *like an invoked god.*

◆ *Old Man Gonsaku at Sea*

Old Man Gonsaku sat opposite me on a chair at the kitchen table. The kitchen was the only room in the house with chairs. It was a very hot evening and he wore just a vest over his trousers, through which you could see the protrusion of his navel. He had a hand towel (*tenugui*) tied around his head, which pushed his hair straight up. His face shone with a thin film of sweat in the dim light. Noticing our stacked supper dishes with the skeletons of fish piled on them set him on course for some fishing and seafaring tales.

Looking at the fish bones where they were placed on top of a cupboard, with his head tilted back, he said to the remains, "We used to fish a lot of cod. I was very good at fishing. In the season we had no time to leave the boat, so wives had to bring rice balls to their husbands. We exchanged our cod for rice balls. We unloaded the cod and got rice balls for our meals and sailed out again. In those days at sea we could catch huge numbers of cod, but these days there are no cod in the sea. I don't know why.

"I fished until my forties, and when I was young, we would hang them outside where they would immediately freeze and then dry. Of course, the cod season is in the winter. Dried cod is very tender like tofu when you cook it. We used to salt it. Cod used to be a cheap fish, but do you know how much you have to pay for one cod today? Very expensive!" He suddenly remembered he had a cup of saké in front of him and, picking it up, smiled into it as usual, as though greeting it on its way to his lips.

He did most of the cooking at home and in the summertime he often fished over the bridge beside his house just before lunch time. He would fish until he had caught enough for both his wife and himself and then disappear inside with his catch.

He put down his cup and passed his hand around his face like someone wiping a plate. "I've had a lot of bitter experiences at sea. So many times I would make up my mind not to go back, but as soon as New Year's day had passed I'd forget and go out again.

"Our ship was a big sailing ship. The mast was eight *sun* [approximately ten inches] in diameter. It only had one mast. No engine. We needed the right wind to cross the bay. A north wind to sail to the other side, and to sail back home, a south wind. Sometimes we had to wait as much as ten days for the right wind. When we had the right one we could sail so fast! It took only two hours to reach the other side. We were faster than boats with engines." He had become very excited. At one point he suddenly leaned forward waving his arm and stood up, just at the same moment that a white moth suddenly appeared over the table. At first I thought he was trying to catch it, but he was reaching for the tiller, wrestling with it. The wind and the sea were making so much noise we could not hear clearly what he was saying, he was so breathless.

From where he had stood up to allow his body to manifest the memory, the wind suddenly dropped him back onto the chair again, and the frothing ocean and the bounding ship dissolved back into the domestic dock of the kitchen. He emptied his cup in one mouthful and I refilled it. "By the way, did you eat the *fuki* (coltsfoot) I gave you yesterday? Did you like it? My old *babā* and I picked it from the footpaths between the rice fields and boiled it. Each year in the early summer we boil it and salt it so we can keep it for a long time and eat it through the year."

We were all silent for a while, and he took a noisy gulp from his cup. Somewhere, a *karakami* opened and closed in a neighboring house. A cat complained from beneath the house next-door. Then, addressing the tape recorder as though it had suddenly occurred to him that here was an opportunity for identifying and recording himself for posterity, he said in a very formal tone, "My name is Fukada Gonsaku. Fu-ka-da Gon-sa-ku eighty-two years old this September. I'm a *jijī* (old man)." He relaxed again, the formal business over with, and giggled like the call-sign of the usual Old Man Gonsaku returning. Back in character, he emptied his cup.

As I took up the bottle, he said, "People in the village used to exchange saké cups with each other and drink from them if they wanted to make a parent and child bond between them. In this way we supported each other. Katsuyama's wife exchanged her cup with Sawada's mother, the mother of the owner of this house, because Katsuyama's wife came from Toyama prefecture and had no relations in the village at all. When Mrs. Sawada was seriously ill, Katsuyama's wife looked after her very well, even though she died in the end. But these days, such a thing has gone. The village is changing. The most obvious thing is that there are no thatched houses anymore, except the gate of the Hosoki family house. And some houses were rebuilt. But mine wasn't."

Masako said it was sad that the temple family, the Tanis, were moving away. "Speaking of the temple family . . ." He was wiping his face again and the words came out from behind his hand. "Taikan [Rev. Tani] used to play on my lap. One time he peed on me." He giggled, "You know, he is now a great monk, and his wife comes from Mawaki. When Taikan first asked her to marry him, she refused him. Anyway, as you know, they're moving to Nakai. Do you think they will really move there?" he asked, looking at us, and then as if to answer himself, "They need money to edu-cate their children. . . . I can remember when most monks in the area traveled around begging, maybe once a month."

He swallowed some more saké, which met the next topic bubbling up from his belly. "I used to make char-coal. I made it myself. I went to my *babā*'s parents' house when I made charcoal. I built a charcoal kiln and slept beside it.

"First of all I dug a hole in the ground." He picked up a

round wooden pot stand that was on the table and used it to describe the hole. "And put wood into it. Then I put twigs and grass over the wood, and then covered it with mud. I lit it and hit the top of it from time to time. When I did this at the beginning, black smoke came out from the airhole, which was like a chimney. When white smoke came out it was a sign that it was ready. My throat could taste the smoke. Black smoke tasted bitter and white smoke tasted completely different. It was lighter. You can taste the difference between saké and water, can't you? Yes, something like that. White smoke was like saké. When I saw the white smoke, I gradually stopped the burning. The best trees for charcoal are trees with acorns.

"When charcoal is still hot, it's soft. But when it cools down, it's so hard you can walk on the kiln. I slept for two or three nights beside the kiln. In those days I did everything myself."

He pulled down on the lobe of his right ear, "About thirty years ago there was a flood in the Anamizu area. It was terrible! In Sora the damage wasn't too bad. Even so, water came up to the floor in my house. It was awful!"

There was another silence while Old Man Gonsaku was engaged with his cup, and I wondered if he was trying to think of another subject to talk about. I rewound the tape a little and played it back. He stared intently at the tiny speaker from where his voice emerged. It was obvious by the expression on his face that he had never heard his voice before.

After the tape had played to the point where I had switched it off, he giggled with an expression of pleasure on his face. "I thought my talking was no good. But listening to my own voice from the machine, it isn't too bad . . . a very good voice!" His body danced the giggles up from his belly and he turned his attention to his cup and peering into it asked, "Am I drinking saké?"

"Yes, it's saké."

"Saké's white, but this is a little bit red." He pointed at the saké in his cup. In fact, he was right. It was the color of the cup through the saké that he was looking at. At home he usually drank saké straight from a small glass, he told us. In fact he was referring to the "One Cup" glasses of saké that he bought at the local farmers' co-op. I explained that it was the color of the cup, which was pottery, and I showed him the color of the saké in my own glass. He sighed, "I began to wonder whether this was real saké or not. But I'm drunk anyway."

"Do you know," Masako said "that you were the first person we met when we came to look at this house? You came out of your house and said, 'I don't know who you are. What are you doing here?'"

"Really? Was I that person?

"Next year I'm going to hold the fiftieth memorial service for my father. I want to invite you both. I am very fond of you. We will have a nice time and chat some more. You will meet my son-in-law who will inherit my family name and who is looking after us. My father died fifty years ago, and my mother died thirty-three years ago.

"One of my daughters is married to a man in Iwagaruma, the next village to Kanami, and they are living there. And the other daughter and her family are living in Kabuto. Their son is a journalist. A journalist writes something for the newspapers, doesn't he?"

It was getting late. I noticed that the light in Yukiko's house next-door had gone out. But Old Man Gonsaku still seemed in full flow. "The vermilion bridge, Kamidebashi, used to be a wooden bridge. As more cars came through the village, it was replaced by the concrete one, which you can now see. Its name is Kamidebashi. I know another Kamidebashi in Morohashi."

He was being blown along by saké. "Years ago there were no houses beyond my house. When some houses were built there, we started to call that side of the village

Kamide. I don't know why. I don't think the old bridge had a name. Maybe the new bridge was named after that side of the village."

We explained that we had been told Kamidebashi meant "bridge where the kami appears."

"No, its *kanji* [Chinese characters] don't mean that. They mean simply "upper bridge.""

He finished his saké and peered into the cup, refusing a refill, saying that he had had his daily quota. He yawned, "We have no rice fields anymore. We used to have some but we gave them to one of my daughters. We kept some vegetable patches for ourselves, though."

He yawned for a second time and we moved toward the *genkan*. He seemed to be back at sea again. The wind had gotten up and the deck was beginning to move beneath his feet. He giggled as he pushed the walls of the corridor away from himself. When we opened the *genkan* door, it was a clear starlit night. The tide was waving its way up the river with a salty bouquet on its fingers.

◆ A Prayer on the Road

One day, returning on foot from Kabuto where I had visited the grocery store, I noticed farther down the road in the direction of Sora the distant figure of a woman standing in the road. She had stopped in the road opposite where the small track turned off leading to Helmet Mountain. As I proceeded toward her, I saw her clap her hands together and bow twice in the direction of the hill and realized she was praying to the kami enshrined at the top. As I drew close to her, I recognized her as Mrs. Nagao's sister. We bowed and greeted each other. I asked her the customary "*Ogenki desu ka?*" [Are you well?], and she told me she was on her way to the clinic in Kabuto. I wished her good health and we continued in our opposite directions.

As always, I was moved by this simple act of faith, an

act that to so many in our so-called culture would appear superstitious and ridiculous. We have become so inflated in our imagined superiority that we think and live as though we are the ones who are in control of our own destinies and the environment in which we live. We have forgotten, it would seem, that we are supported all the while by both the visible and the invisible in the universe and that the living and intelligent pulse of the cosmos is one of interdependence and reciprocity. We have forgotten simple gratitude—to thank other manifestations of being and their different energies with whom we share this time/space, whether animate or inanimate, for their support. We have forgotten how to ask—we just take (for granted, and more than we need) without return. Whereas, for people like the people of Sora, recognition of and homage to the environment is a natural, unselfconscious day-to-day expression of their own being, whether to the numerous Shintō kami or to Buddha (a distinction that they often do not bother to make).

It is even more ironic that in the present state of our imagined superiority we style ourselves "human beings," when it is we on this planet who have forgotten what "being" means.

◆ Stone Buddha Mountain (Ishibotoke Yama)

One late summer afternoon, we were driving through a village when we saw a weatherbeaten sign that bore an arrow and the words "Ishibotoke Yama." We were so intrigued by the name that we decided to investigate and drove down a narrow track beside some rice fields and into a small forested valley. About half a mile farther on, the track began to fade into a forest path, as the valley narrowed, and on the right rose the steep forested side of a large hill. Here we came across another weatherworn sign, though much larger than the first. This indicated a path up the forested hillside, but added a prohibition on the access of women to the hill. We parked the car at the end of the track and retraced our steps, the whole valley reverberating with the voices of cicadas. Masako decided that in light of the regulations stipulated on the board she would rather walk beside the rice fields. So I set off up the steep path on my own.

After walking for ten minutes or so up through the forest beside a stream that the path followed, I came across a rice-straw rope with white zigzag paper streamers attached to it lying on the ground. This rope is called a *shimenawa* and indicates the boundary of, or entrance to, the temenos or sacred area, which is the abode of a kami. It must have fallen from where it would have been attached, hanging between two trees or pieces of bamboo set in the ground. Here I paused and clapped my hands together twice, in the same manner as one would at a Shintō shrine, and then stepped over the *shimenawa*.

Suddenly, either through suggestion prompted by the sight of the *shimenawa* or a genuine apprehension of a change in the environmental ambiance, or a combination of these, I became aware of a presence. Rather than a single presence, there was a palpable feeling of the charge of the whole environment of that place—the collective presence of each rock, fungus, tree, etc. For a moment, I had the distinct impression that I was being observed, not by any one thing but by everything.

Then, passing around the trunk of a huge tree, I saw it—a giant standing stone in a small clearing amongst massive trees. Pale lichen and striations of white in the stone gave it the appearance of glowing in the late afternoon gloom. There was a rice-straw rope thicker than the first *shimenawa*, with white paper strips hanging from it, tied around its girth, denoting the stone's sacred nature. Planted in the ground in front of the stone was the weathered remains of a *gohei*, a wand with white paper again folded in zigzags and used as a symbolic offering and also to indicate the presence of a kami. On either side of this huge stone was a much smaller stone, so that the whole presented a very obvious phallic form.

Though in a much different form, it immediately reminded me of the Giant of Cerne Abbas with his huge penis and great phallic club, whose linear image is cut into the chalk on a hill overlooking the village of Cerne Abbas in Dorset. He is thought to have been a kind of agricultural Hercules, anyway, a god of fertility. A girl-friend of mine had lived at the foot of this hill, and I remembered climbing it to examine the site with her. Unfortunately, but perhaps properly, she became pregnant soon afterward!

From the name "Stone Buddha Mountain," I had been expecting a Buddhist site of some kind, not a very primitive and early Shintō one. On reflection, however, I realized that its name indicated the period soon after Buddhism began to establish itself in Japan, when an alliance was formed between Buddhism and Shintō.

It was obvious by what I found on Stone Buddha Mountain that some form of worship and ritual still regularly took place there, and I was very interested to find out more about it. As I got into the car, where Masako was waiting, she asked me what I had found up there. "It's extraordinary," I said, and explained what I had seen. "We have to come back again. And next time you must come up with me."

◆ Temple Cleaning and the Bodhisattvas of the Bandages

During the spring and summer months, I took the advantage of opening all the windows and doors in the temple to keep it aired throughout. While I worked about the place, I was often observed by a kite that would sit high in the great *shii* oak that stood in front of the temple at the top of the steps. I would call up at it some days, and it would mew down at me, as though we shared some gossip or other.

One such day, when the weather was like living in the outskirts of some kind of heaven, I had opened the main doors to the Buddha hall and decided to spring-clean the altars. Besides the main altar devoted to Kannon, there were three other altars. To the right of the main altar was an image of Kōbō Daishi, the founder of the sect, and to the left of the main altar was an ancient wooden image of Jizō seated in the lotus position. On the far left, in its own area of the hall, a large altar stood, crowded with images, funerary tablets, and scrolls of various kinds. This altar was dedicated to those whose ashes were interred in the temple graveyard, and many of the images had once belonged to the deceased's own household altars.

While I was moving the various ritual objects and images around in order to clean them, I was suddenly reminded of a time some years earlier, when we had visited my father-in-law in the hospital. While we were turned out of the ward so that some procedure or examination could be carried out, we sat in a waiting area already occupied by two *yakuza* (Japanese gangsters). They had obviously left their respective wards for a smoke. One was in his early to mid-sixties and obviously of a reasonably high rank, smoking his cigarette in an artistically long holder and wearing what looked like lizard-skin slippers, with his silk dressing gown thrown casually over his shoulders. He reminded me of a cross between a Japanese version of Somerset Maugham and a sick Hollywood Mafia boss, the latter being perhaps the more likely image he wished to project. Sitting with him was a young foot soldier with the obligatory sawn-off pinkie, which he proudly displayed during our conversation. His torso and head were swathed in bandages, and it transpired that he had been using an oxyacetylene torch when, through some faulty connection, the whole business had blown up, setting him on fire. He complained that his boss had angrily refused to accept his reason for not jumping out of the way—he was standing on scaffolding six floors up at the time!

As he spoke to me, I at first thought I was beginning to hallucinate. Looking at his eyes between the gaps in his bandaged head, while he spoke I kept receiving flashes of the face of Kannon floating somewhere around his right shoulder. It was some moments before I could reasonably disengage my eyes from his, without giving away that I was seeing something more interesting, and inspect the area of my apparent transcendental vision. There, to my relief but utter amazement, was indeed the face of Kannon. But that was not all. From various other gaps in the bandaging covering his torso, the faces and hands and odd bits of clothing and adornments of a whole entourage of bodhisattvas and celestial minders appeared and disappeared, as though ascending a holy mountain through mystical cloud.

Suddenly, summoned to time and place by what I quickly interpreted to be a question as to the number of girlfriends I had had, I did a rough calculation, while at the same time thinking what an odd question it was. On releasing my reply, they had both reacted with an identical, extended "Haaaaaaaaa!" and then bowing deeply and possibly painfully, their behavior had changed from curiosity to great deference and respect. The young foot soldier even began to unwind his bandages so that I could gain a better view of the august and holy company that journeyed about his epidermis. He explained that the only thing that had worried him when he was burning was the state of his insurance coverage on his tattoos, which must have cost him a small fortune.

It had only been later that evening when I asked Masako, who had been sitting a few yards away observing the conversation, about some of the Japanese used that their change in behavior was explained. The *yakuza* and I had apparently completely misunderstood each other. My reply to what I thought had been a question concerning the number of girlfriends I had known, had been understood as the number of women that I managed. They thought I was a British pimp!

While I had been working in the Buddha hall, recalling the above and at the same time trying to concentrate very carefully on my work, in order to remember the exact order and position of the ritual objects that were laid out in an area in front of the main altar, I had not noticed how dark the hall had suddenly become. I went outside and stood in the porch looking up at the sky. It was heavy and cloud-covered. It looked metallic and loaded, except at the horizon of the sea, below which a bright light gave the illusion that the end of the sea stood up vertically like a wall. The waters before it were black, purple, and flat, like wet asphalt. The kite, high in its tree, mewed fretfully, making me look up at it.

I had just gone up to my workroom to check that the windows were closed, when the sky unloaded itself with a bright artery of blue fire that seemed to catch the top of the sea's wall and throw it down. In the brief rush that accompanied that atmospheric charge, the whole horizon had become neoned so fast that the perceptual moment of its ignition could only be reviewed in the freeze-flash behind closed eyelids. Then, stammering and slamming like a train over a bridge, the breath of its path sent the air in the room shunting against my eardrums. The thunder rolled from one end of the sky to the other, then seemed to break up into sound-bites that grumbled intermittently for some minutes somewhere along the borders of the late afternoon where it met evening.

As I turned to go back down into the hall, there was another bright flash, as though someone with a huge cloud-camera were taking snapshots and then rolling the sky on to the next exposure. The vibration caused by each shock made the whole structure of the old temple flinch, so that its great timbers groaned under the weight of its huge roof.

I decided to return home before the rain came and quickly lit some incense at the altar and checked that I had left everything in order. As I took my bicycle out of the shelter, large drops began to fall, bruising the broad, flat stone in front of the Jizō images at the foot of the temple steps. The flat surface of the sea a few feet in front of me was beginning to pucker all over, as though thousands of tiny mouths were sucking at the sky from just beneath its surface.

The street was empty as I cycled back down it, except for a few parked tractors and a family of black-and-white cats seeking shelter beneath one of the houses. As I crossed the vermilion bridge and turned left to our house, a heron rose up on a shriek, releasing the river from its feet and embracing the thickening rain in its wings.

On the kitchen table there was a letter from Shorō, a friend of mine who is a priest of the Jōdo Shin sect of the Pure Land School of Buddhism, enclosing his temple's circular and inviting us to the *hōonkō*, the memorial services for the great thirteenth-century priest Shinran, founder of the sect.

> *Frenetic thunder,*
> *manic lightning*
> *and ecstatic crickets*
> *—moon and trees*
> *in their single stillness.*

◆ A Gift of Three Plants

It was a muggy, energyless day in the rainy season, but there had been little rain as yet and the earth was thirsting. We were outside weeding the small patch at the back of the house beside the barn when I heard footsteps crossing over the small bridge to our house. Looking up, I saw Old Man Gonsaku coming toward us. As he saw me look up, he called out and giggled. As he squatted down beside us he said, and it was obvious, that he had drunk a bit of saké.

He began telling us what an interesting child he had been. Then we told him what an interesting old man he was now. He sat watching us pulling the weeds for a while, and then getting up said he was going to give us something. He returned over the bridge to his house.

He came back ten minutes later with three eggplant plants in his hand. He sat cross-legged on the ground and began to dig holes for them with a trowel. After making sure they were well bedded in, he stood up and looked up and down the river. Without any bidding or apparent reason, he suddenly pulled up his vest and displayed his belly. It bore a huge scar like the relief of a vapor trail fashioned in flesh, where the turbulence of a knife had left its track.

"You had a baby?" I asked laughing.

"Yes, all my grandchildren came out from here." He pulled his vest down again with a giggle, and explained that he had had an operation. As he began to describe the surgical process, an old woman of eighty-four, who lived on the street behind our house, passed along the track that ran beside our house along the bank of the river. As she crossed over the small bridge, Old Man Gonsaku called out after her, "You're a very attractive woman! Beautiful!"

Without turning around, she shouted back, "Idiot!"

"You are," he replied, with his head tilted back, looking after her. Then to us, "She's a very attractive woman. In order to live a long life, sexual attraction is very important. And you must eat everything and not say you don't like this or that." Giggling, he shuffled off across the bridge in the direction of his own house.

A few minutes later Mrs. Kitayama, the headman's

wife, joined us with a gift of some vegetables from her patch, and we stood talking, when Old Man Gonsaku reappeared for the third time and joined us, carrying what looked like a framed picture. It turned out to be a large framed photograph of his two grandsons, the ones he had mentioned to us when we had joked about his belly.

The glass was filthy and flyblown so I took it into the house and cleaned it for him. When I handed it back to him, he expressed amazement at how different his grandsons looked. "I hang it at the same level as the television, because you only hang photos of the dead high on the wall." He held it up at eye-level.

Setting the photograph down on the ground, he suddenly bowed to Masako. "Your husband is from Great Britain. Headman's wife is from another village. *Okusan* (wife, referring to Masako herself) is from Tokyo. I'm from Sora. These people I love."

"You love yourself?" asked Mrs. Kitayama grinning.

"Well, I'm not a bad man."

"I remember when you were young you drank a lot of saké and got angry and took all your clothes off and lay in the middle of the road, showing your prick to everyone."

"Of course! When I took my trousers off, how could I hide it?"

We dispersed in laughter to our respective kitchens.

◆ Weeping Timber

A friend, whose job it had been to select different qualities of wood at a sawmill until he became blind in his forties, was sitting with us in our house one afternoon. I happened to comment on the amount of resin that had oozed out of the wood in our house since it had been built. He explained that the resin was the "wood's tears," and that it should have been cleaned with saké after the house was built to make it "calm down."

◆ A *Domestic* **Incident**

One night, having drunk too much saké, I was sitting on the riverbank outside the house when I heard the sounds of an argument coming from Old Man Gonsaku's. The shouting became louder, as someone had obviously moved out from the interior of the house into the *genkan* and was trying to open the door. But the door seemed to have jammed. After much shaking and shouting, it slid open an inch or so and the fingers of a hand appeared, clasping the frame. Finally, the door slammed open and Old Man Gonsaku emerged, made a few staggering circles in the road outside the house, as though his body-compass was confused, and then set off over the bridge shouting in the spotlight of the street lamp.

A few moments later, the cat flew out of the *genkan* into the road, pursued by Mrs. Fukada, shouting and gesticulating at it. It skidded sharply to the right and took refuge behind a metal ladder that was lying lengthwise against the front wall. Mrs. Fukada sat down on an old office-swivel chair that she kept outside the door and stared hard into the darkness up and down the road.

Suddenly, Old Man Gonsaku reappeared on the bridge out of the darkness, like the ghost in a Noh play, crossing the bridge between this realm and the next. Mrs. Fukuda leapt up from the chair as though it had suddenly become electrified and disappeared into the house. On reaching the front of the house, Old Man Gonsaku turned a few more circles with his head tilted back, as if about to engage in combat with some unseen adversary. Then, steadying on his feet, he took a piece of pipe that was propped up against the wall beside the *genkan* door and, using it as a walking stick, he lurched over to the ladder. He slid the pipe along the rungs, like a builder's harp, making a hideous but appropriate din as an accompaniment to the drama. It flushed out the cat, which he followed off into the dark shouting, in the opposite direction to the one he had just reappeared from, till the night enfolded him and his anger in its wings.

◆ The Kannon Chant (Kanshugyō)—Boy's Midwinter Discipline

The name of the temple is Senjuin. "Senju" means "one-thousand arms." This refers to the image of Kannon (Ch. Kuan Yin; Skt. Avalokitesvara), the Bodhisattva of Compassion, which is enshrined in the temple, and is the principle focus of worship. It is common for images of this bodhisattva to be depicted with many arms, the hands of which hold various ritual and symbolic objects or make symbolic hand gestures (mudra). One thousand is a number that symbolizes the countless or infinite number of acts of compassion that Kannon performs simultaneously and mindfully without effort in all realms.

Soon after arriving in the village, we were told of an event that was unique to this temple and the village of Sora. It involves house-to-house chanting by boys of the village in the depths of winter in order to collect alms to buy candles for the temple. We had inquired about its nature and origins, but most people seemed to know very little about it, save for the fact that it had happened every year since they could remember. Added to this, many villagers, even those who must have taken part as boys themselves, were very shy to express themselves or assume any knowledge. The general consensus seemed to be that we should ask Mr. Muroki, who lived in a house just outside the main village on the road toward the village of Kanami. He had apparently written an article about it in the local town magazine some years previously.

Mr. Muroki lived alone, as his wife had died a few years ago. He was now eighty-three and partially disabled by a degenerative condition of the lower vertebrae. This meant that he needed the assistance of two sticks in order to move around, although this in no way seriously impeded his activities around his house and garden, or the village, or even the local town to which he traveled on a small motorbike.

When we first visited him and inquired about *kanshugyō* (literally, "winter discipline"), he had suggested that he visit us the following week. The morning he was due to come, Masako had prepared lunch for him to take back to his house, as he had told us on receiving the invitation that he always preferred to eat meals at home.

At about nine-thirty I heard his motorbike outside and watched him as he moved laboriously across the small bridge to our house. On seeing me as I slid the front door open, his face lit up with a smile and we greeted each other. He came into the *genkan* sideways, manipulating his sticks while turning to sit on the step into the main house to remove his shoes. He remarked on the weather as he laid one of his sticks, a wooden one, in a corner and put on a pair of slippers. Then, smiling, he followed me along the corridor with the help of the remaining stick, a black metal telescopic one, to a room at the end of the house next to the kitchen.

As we sat on the tatami waiting for Masako to bring in some coffee, which we had learned was his passion, he looked around the room, commenting on and admiring pieces of Masako's needlework and black-ink paintings (*sumi-e*) that hung about the walls. I, in the meantime, prepared my notebook and checked the sound level on the tape recorder.

Mr. Muroki did not speak with a Sora dialect because he had spent a great deal of his life away from the village where he had been born. When he spoke of anything of a serious nature, he adopted a very formal, schoolmaster-ish delivery, which, it occurred to me afterward, may have been due to the presence of the tape recorder.

When we were all settled with our coffees, he cleared his throat and began, "In spite of its long tradition, no one knows anything about the origin of *kanshugyō* because no records of any history exist. But we do know the practice has gone on for generations. It started a long time ago—we believe at least as far back as the Edo period (1603–1868), because the bell that is used in the chanting was, according to the date on it, cast at that time.

"More than twenty years ago, the people from NHK |the national broadcasting company| heard of this spiritual discipline for boys and wanted to film it. They asked us about its origins and so on. At that time we decided to write a small piece about this discipline. Two old men of the village and I put together our memories and also whatever we had been told by our fathers and grandfathers. What I'm about to tell you is based on that article, which I also contributed to the local town magazine.

"Winter *shugyō* is a kind of discipline for boys who reach ten or eleven years of age. Before the war, that was the age at which you finished compulsory education. In those days it was often extended to fourteen or fifteen years of age. Even so, today only primary-school boys are allowed to participate in this *shugyō*.

"In the Edo period our village was directly governed by the Tokugawa shogunate and not by the local lord, which meant that all land taxes of rice were paid directly to the shogunate. In those days people made their living only by farming, fishing, and making salt. I've heard that back then everyone had enough to live on. Even so, there was a custom called *kuchiberashi* |literally, "reducing the number of mouths"|, when children who had reached a certain age or finished their primary-school education had to leave home and go away to work.

"In our village here we only have one temple, Senjuin of the Shingon sect. That was where the children went to school, and its compound was their playground. Con-

sequently, any experience connected with the temple
was exciting and precious to us. I can remember being
very excited picking up the small, round rice cakes that
were scattered by the monk after the special service in
March called *nehan* [celebrating the historical Buddha
Shakyamuni's death and his final liberation from the
cycles of rebirth (Parinirvana)]. We called these rice cakes
nehan dango [Nirvana cakes] and we placed them in small
bags and kept them in our pockets for protection against
poisonous snakes. If we became sick, we would grind up
the cakes and swallow them. We still believe it works."

At this point someone opened the *genkan* door and
called out, "Okusan!" (Mrs.). Masako got up from the
table and went down the passage to the *genkan*. I could
hear that it was the headman's wife. She was obviously
giving something to Masako. Later I discovered that Mrs.
Kitayama had brought some wild vegetables she had collected from the mountainside early that morning.

While Masako was at the *genkan*, Mr. Muroki turned to
his coffee, which he had left untouched till now. "Mmmm.
Delicious," he said with a grin. Then as Masako reseated
herself he continued, "Another unforgettable event was
Buddha's birthday [April 8]. We always looked forward to
joining in on these occasions.

"Do you know, there is a huge *shii* tree in front of the
Buddha hall? In autumn we used to pick up its acorns.
They tasted very, very sweet. You see how precious our
memories connected with the temple are?

"Thinking about the origins of *kanshugyō*, I can easily
imagine that one particular year the boys probably wanted to do something for the temple and the monk in order
to express their thanks and appreciation and at the same
time prepare for their unknown futures, before they left
their families and the village. I think the idea became a
kind of *shugyō* for themselves, in order to return the kindness to the temple and at the same time to discipline

their own minds and bodies. Since then, this *shugyō* has continued and has become a kind of duty for the boys in our village."

Masako put down her coffee cup. "Why was it only for boys?"

"I don't know, I don't know why it was only for boys. As you know, the population of this village is declining, and of course there are fewer children. In fact, when my daughter was nine or ten, she was asked to join them. She was very surprised but delighted. After this, as far as I can remember, they somehow managed to carry on with just boys, but only by allowing in younger boys. But they never invited boys from another village, even if they were desperately needed."

He paused, and taking up his metal walking stick with its large, black rubber ferrule, he prodded at something either actual or imaginary, but anyway invisible to me, on the tatami beside where he was sitting. And as he then turned and sipped his by-now-cold coffee, I found myself looking at the flesh on the right side of his face in the area where his hair and the joint of his jawbone met. The skin there was orangy and mottled, a beautiful mellow color, like the skin of a late autumn apple.

He set his cup down again. "On the evening of the first day of the cold season, we gathered at the temple. One of us carried the chant bell, one a six-sided candle lantern, and one bags for collecting donations, which would either be money or rice or something.

"We all sat in front of Kannon-sama in the Buddha hall to have a short service, and the monk chanted. After that, in my day, the village women began *go-eika* [a special form of chanting with small bells]. While they chanted, we set off to call at all the houses in the village. Walking and chanting with the sound of the bell, we approached the first house. In front of the house, the boy carrying the bell hit it twice and the rest of us chanted *Namu Daishi Kanzeon*.

Then one of us would quietly slide the *genkan* door open, and the bell was hit twice again. In time, someone would appear with something in their hand and say with a smile, "*Gokurōsan*" [Thank you for your effort]. One of us would open his bag and receive rice or money. Then we would all chant *Namu Daishi Kanzeon*, and the bell would be rung twice again. We then gave our thanks and bowed, closing the *genkan* door and moving along to the next house.

"Hearing the sound of the bell approaching, some people would already be waiting for us outside their houses. And some people gave us grilled rice cakes to eat. In this way we visited about eighty houses.

"When we returned to the temple, we reentered the Buddha hall with the women chanting *go-eika* again. Then we were invited to eat *zenzai* [thick, sweet red-bean broth], which warmed our frozen bodies. We repeated this same pattern for seven evenings.

"It was really the coldest time of the year. I remember during one *shugyō* we had a snowstorm and piercing winds off the sea. The weather wasn't helpful at all, which really indicates the hardship of *shugyō*. Some of us wore rice-straw capes and boots."

There was a pause while he drained his cup and declined another. A heron shrieked outside the window, its shadow climbing up over the roof. Someone must have been passing by on the road outside. He drew the back of his hand across his mouth, "On the completion of our round of seven evenings, we counted all our donations. Whatever we could sell, I mean rice, we sold for cash in order to buy candles to dedicate to Kannon.

"Dedicated candles were lit on the evening of January 17 in front of the altar containing the image of Kannon. Listening to the monk chanting, we thought over all our experiences during the seven cold evenings. And as he ended his chanting with the sound of the bell, all our tension was released and replaced with joy at having accomplished *shugyō*, along with all the complicated feelings of having to leave home and the village.

"After this service, we were all invited to supper. Before we started, the monk gave us a talk and expressed his appreciation for the candles. Sitting and chatting cheerfully, our minds were filled with the confidence and joy that we would get through the first trial of our life. I am sure all the boys and men in the village share this memory of a cold, hard but precious *shugyō*.

"The whole business is organized and carried out by the boys themselves. Adults never interfere in their decisions. The boys take responsibility for everything. I think it's very special and unusual.

"Not all the families in the village belong to Senjuin, which means that their own temples (of various sects) are in other villages. For example, my family temple is on Noto Island and belongs to the Jōdo Shin sect. But everyone is willing to cooperate in the boys' *shugyō*. I believe it's this supportive attitude that is the main reason why we have been keeping this tradition alive in this village." He smiled, drawing his hand down over his face, nodding to himself, as though happily approving all that he had heard himself telling.

As he crossed back over the small bridge from our house, we walked behind him, carrying his lunch and concerned that he should not slip or stumble over into the river. He slid both his sticks under some elasticized ties on the rack at the back of his motorbike, and with one hand on the bike to support himself he removed his helmet from the tank where he had left it and flipped it over the back of his head till it settled down on his skull. I had difficulty in restraining myself from assisting him onto the saddle, but realized this actually would neither be necessary nor helpful, since it was an operation he had to carry out several times a day and by himself.

When he opened the throttle at the vermilion bridge,

the bike skidded slightly as he turned right onto the road for his home.

◆ *Entertaining the Kami of the Rice Field (Aenokoto)*

In certain areas of Noto there is a period during the winter, when families mainly affiliated with the Shingon sect of Buddhism entertain the Shintō kami of their rice fields. These kami are personal to the particular families whose rice fields they protect, since most are understood to be ancestors of these families and are usually thought to be a couple. The ceremonial form this entertainment takes varies slightly from family to family, so that represented here is a composite of several such families' *aenokoto*.

On the morning of December 5, the house is thoroughly cleaned and swept, and at three o'clock in the afternoon the head of the family dresses formally in kimono and *hakama* (men's culottes) and *kamishimo* (a top traditionally worn by samurai for formal occasions). On the previous day, he would have gone to a nearby mountain to choose and cut a young, sweet chestnut tree in order to make chopsticks for the kami. But first he would address the kami of the mountain by saying, "Kami of the Mountain, may I cut this young sweet chestnut to make chopsticks for tomorrow's *aenokoto*?" He would then take the tree home and fashion chopsticks from it.

Now, dressed as described above, he goes to his rice field carrying his oldest hoe (*kuwa*). He digs the hoe into the soil, lifting a sod containing rice stubble in which the kami are believed to reside, and claps his hands twice and addresses the kami, "Rice field kami, I have come to see you to thank you for your great effort." He then carries the stubble sod containing the kami back to his house and places it on the household Shintō shrine. Next, he prepares a feast in the guest room on two small lacquer tables. Great care is taken in the preparation of each aspect of this meal, as clumsiness could have disastrous consequences and result in a bad harvest the following year. The feast varies again from family to family but typically consists of the following small dishes: rice mixed with red beans; tofu soup; a mix comprising cooked daikon radish, carrot, burdock, taro yam, grilled tofu, seaweed, and herring; grilled fish; raw herring; pickled yellowtail and daikon radish. Also presented before these two tables, but not as part of the meal, are two raw daikon radishes, each with bifurcated roots, making them look like two naked bodies. In some households the kami will bathe before the meal, in others afterward.

The kami are then shown into the guest room and the head of the family bows respectfully before the two tables and bids the kami to enjoy their meal. After a reasonable time, the head of the family reenters the room and invites the kami to enter the bathhouse, where a hot bath has been drawn for them.

Once it is considered that enough time has elapsed to enable the kami to have bathed well, the kami are shown back to the shrine, where they will rest for the duration of the winter.

At the end of the winter, on the morning of February 9 or thereabouts, the head of the family will go to the mountain and choose a young pine tree, which he ritually cuts after seeking the permission of the kami of the mountain. He then carries the pine down to his home, where he places it in a straw bag filled with seed-rice. He then prepares a feast similar to the one prepared in December, complete with chopsticks of sweet chestnut, except this time offered before each of the lacquer tables is a daikon radish with a straight, single root in contrast to the forked roots of the ones presented in December.

Once the feast is considered to be perfectly prepared, the kami are conducted from the Shintō shrine to the guest room, where the feast is laid, and moved into the pine tree, where the head of the family addresses them and invites them to enjoy the food that has been prepared for them.

After the feast, the kami are invited to bathe before being escorted back to the rice field. In the case of one family, the kami are said to be blind, due to the heads of the rice remaining in the ground one year and damaging their eyes. In this case, everything is explained and described verbally to them.

After the kami have returned to the pine tree, the head of the family takes his oldest hoe to the rice field, where he makes an offering before it of a rice cake shaped in the form of a hoe. He then returns to the house and carries the kami in the pine tree to the rice field, where he addresses them again, "Kami of the rice field, we will do our best. We will not be defeated by the weather, worms, insects, or drought. We pray for a good harvest." Then breaking the ground in three places in front of the pine tree with the old hoe, the kami are invited to reenter the rice field. And so another agricultural year commences.

◆ The New Bicycle

Old Man Gonsaku had bought himself a new white bicycle. It stood shining outside his house. White is the color of purification (it used to be the color of death) and, in Japan, a color for protection; and still most vehicles in the countryside are traditionally white.

As I looked across at the bicycle from my workroom window, the front door of his house opened and he emerged. He stood for some moments on the lower step and looked at his new machine. Then he stepped up onto the road and walked around it, staring at it and occasionally tilting his head back to look up and down the road. He moved toward the bike and laid his hand gently on the saddle. Standing at arm's length before moving forward, he placed his left hand on the left grip of the handlebars and stooped to examine something near the front forks. Then, releasing the kickstand with his foot, he wheeled it across to the fire-equipment shed where his old, dirty white bicycle stood up against the wall.

He stood his new bicycle alongside it, as though introducing them. He took several paces back and looked at them, obviously comparing them. After a few moments he turned away and looked toward his house with his head tilted back but then swiveled his head sharply back to look at his new bicycle again. I wondered if he was trying to cancel the visual memory of it by distracting himself in order to suddenly see it afresh, as if for the first time, through vision emptied of any reference. In any event, he stood stock still, as though stunned by its beauty.

Suddenly, after standing like this for some time, he walked around the new bicycle and then got down on the ground between it and the old one. He looked from one to the other, lightly touching the tire of one and then the tire of the other, talking to himself or to them all the while. Looking at each of them from different angles, he patted and carressed them, as though they were two living beings and even though it had become necessary for one to be put out to grass, he still expressed gratitude and love toward it.

This apparent introducing of the new bicycle and the comforting of the old lasted for about half an hour, till all sides seemed satisfied and secure in the change of circumstance. He mounted his new shining steed and rode off in the direction of the farmers' co-op, no doubt for a celebratory glass or two of saké.

◆ A *Temple* Visit

When the time arrived for the three-day *hōonkō* service on the anniversary of the death of Shinran, founder of the

Jōdo Shin sect, we set about plans to visit our priest friend, Shorō, who lives in a temple near Lake Biwa. On previous occasions when I had visited on my own, I had always stayed in the temple in a room behind the Buddha hall that overlooked a rice field. This time, however, it was decided that we should stay in an empty house in the village not far from the temple. We decided that we would drive the three hundred-odd miles there, since we would have to carry all our own cooking pots and food supplies for the two-week stay.

After greetings and a cup of tea at the temple, we were taken to a large house backing onto rice fields with a traditional stone garden, featuring a dry river with a dry waterfall and stone lantern. It had been owned by a couple who both died of cancer within a few days of each other. In the room containing the Buddhist altar there was a separate shrine set up to both these people, with an incense burner, flowers, candles, and large framed photographs of each. The shrine was regularly attended to by one of their relations who lived in the village and took responsibility for the house. It was he who had generously agreed to allow us to stay in it, since our business was connected with the temple.

Quite apart from the presence of the shrine, we both experienced a deathful atmosphere permeating the entire house, though perhaps under the circumstances that was to be expected. The room we were instructed was to be our bedroom was on the ground floor next to the room with the Buddhist altar and had once belonged to the wife. The atmosphere was particularly strong here and heightened by the presence of thirty-three small dolls suspended from the ceiling, which hung like a platoon of miniature parachutists frozen in mid-fall. It made the room look as though it had been used for some strange kind of ritual. Behind *karakami* that divided off the window end of the room into what once had been the wife's dressing room, there was a dressing table with a variety of bottles and small lidded boxes on its surface. Various pieces of clothing still hung from the walls on hangers. The room had obviously not been disturbed since the wife's death. It might have been a corner of a Japanese Miss Haversham's boudoir. There was a sickly smell of scented powder or residual perfume in the stagnant air. It felt like a dressing room still frequented by a neurotic ghost.

We did not mention our discomfort to Shorō, however, since it was his constant generosity and kindness that had given me access to priests and temples apart from his own, which I would otherwise not have enjoyed. And in any case, to have said anything would have been extremely bad manners in the face of the open-heartedness expressed by everyone we met in the village and whose support we enjoyed throughout our time there.

That first evening we were invited to a concert in the village hall that was part of the village's cultural week, which included exhibitions, talks, and demonstrations of various kinds. The villagers performed a variety of musical acts and recitations, while bountiful supplies of beer and saké augmented many impromptu performances on the stairs and in the street outside to accompany the events on the main stage.

I am not usually overenthusiastic about performing in public, particularly singing, but being fairly well tuned by both saké and beer and feeling perhaps under some imagined obligation, when asked to sing, I quickly found myself on the stage with a microphone in my hand through which I delivered a slightly numbed version of "She Moves Through the Fair." It has occurred to me since that this particular song may have been subliminally suggested by the atmosphere in the house, since the song describes a spectral visitation.

The following morning, very hung-over, I opened the

back door to find a pile of vegetables lying up against the door. Just as we were commenting on the generosity of our anonymous benefactor, I was hit by the sobering thought that after my performance the previous evening perhaps the vegetables had been thrown where they lay by way of critical comment. This act of kindness, however, was repeated each day of our stay, either in the early morning or the late evening, till we had enough to open a green-grocery business.

After a few days, the atmosphere in the house had become so heavy that we felt we had to be out of it as much as possible. Fortunately, for the first three days, we had to attend the *hōonkō* service at the temple during the day and various meetings and study classes in the evenings, arranged by Shorō. After these three days, we had two free days before we were due to accompany Shorō's father to the *hōonkō* services at two neighboring temples, where he was taking part in the chanting.

On the evening of the last day of the *hōonkō* at Shorō's temple, after we had returned to the house, I lit a candle and burned incense at the Buddhist altar, as I was in the habit of doing at home, and began to chant the *Shōshinge* (the essence of Shin teaching presented in verse form). I was halfway through chanting, when I was suddenly overcome by the most terrible feelings of grief, which threw me down in front of the altar in convulsive and total-body weeping.

This was not the first time I had experienced something like this while sitting in front of someone else's altar. In our house in Sora, the original owner of which had also died of cancer and had been a devout Shin Buddhist, I had been taken over by the *nembutsu* (saying the name of Amida Buddha in the form Namu Amida Butsu) three days in succession, after reopening what had been the original owner's Buddhist altar. As soon as I had lit the candle and the incense and rung the bell, the *nembutsu* flew out of my mouth so fast that my tongue had difficulty keeping up and articulating it.

A night later, I woke with the most appalling feelings of nausea, till I finally vomited and kept vomiting for the whole of the night until the next morning, when I was too weak to get up from the futon. I remained in the futon the entire next day, and it was two days before I felt well enough to venture out.

At any rate, Shorō had informed Masako as to the identity of the provider of the vegetables. He was an old farmer and a devout member of the temple who lived two houses away. We decided to pay him a visit one day and to take a small gift in thanks for his generosity.

As we walked into the yard in front of his house, we were accosted by an ancient-looking dog that was anchored by a piece of rope to a post, which supported the lean-to of a building to the left of the main house. We approached the *genkan* and, sliding open the door, announced our presence to the silent interior of the house, while the dog kept up a repetition of its objection.

After repeating our greeting and still failing to receive any response, I decided to try the door in the building to the left of the house. This meant that in order to reach the door I had to pass the objecting dog. As I slid open the door and again announced our presence, the dog, at full-stretch of the rope, pointed its nose just an inch or so from my leg, so that I could feel the temperature of interior-heat transmitted through the corduroy of my trousers by each bark.

The face of a young man, who had obviously just gotten up from his futon, appeared around the door. He yawned and stretched and I apologized for waking him. Just at that moment, the old farmer appeared, smiling from the *genkan* of the main house. He came over and laid his hand on the dog's convulsing back as it insistently delivered its message and ordered, "Quiet! Don't bite!"

It was as though this last command "Don't bite!" had sprung some hitherto lost or forgotten cerebral connection in some neurological fruit machine and paid out through the canine's reeking maw, as the head contacted my left leg with a brief, gummy clasp and seemed to bounce back off. Then, apparently regrouping scattered reflexes, the dog lunged again, scoring a minor but painful penetration with what appeared to be its only remaining tooth. My own reflexes quickly reacted and pulled my leg out of range, the black corduroy of my trousers snagging on the animals briefly rejuvenated fang, tearing a small hole.

The farmer was very upset and when I explained that it was of no consequence, he did an unusual thing for a Japanese of his generation and background, he embraced me.

The pain of this minor wound dogged me for several days and remained as a small blue dot—a minimalist tattoo—for some weeks. And for the next few days, each time I came to the *hōonkō* services, to sit with my legs folded under my body and chant, I was reminded of the dog's own chanting to dispel foreign devils.

> A *five-hundred-year-old*
> Amida image
> *sits in the* Buddha Hall,
> *while* Buddha's
> *paint-chipped tricycle*
> *stands by the gate*

◆ The Yellow Surplice

One afternoon while we were at Shorō's temple, we were sitting in the reception room just off to one side of the Buddha hall when Shorō's father, Rev. Fukuda senior (called *"Gorosō"* by his wife, a title of respect that simply means "old monk"), came in wearing his usual black priest's robe but with a small yellow hemp *kesa* (surplice) over it, which we had never seen before. The beautiful simplicity of the *kesa* struck us, since many of the priests' *kesa* these days are hugely expensive and elaborate. In fact, I have seen some priests directing special services who look as though they are carrying draylon sofas on their backs! (Though they are in fact made of the finest silk brocade and gold thread.)

When we admired it, he said, "Tomorrow is the anniversary of my father's death, so I put this on today. This small *kesa* is called *gakumon-gesa*, which means 'a *kesa* for studying.' I've got lots of them, but I decided to put this *kesa* on for formal occasions inside our temple."

Masako explained to him her idea for giving abandoned kimono and other types of material new life by making them into wall-hangings, bags, cushion-covers, and so on. She said to Gorosō, "I think your yellow *kesa* is beautiful. May I measure it so I can make a wall-hanging of old cloth to the same measurements?" (A *kesa* is made up of various-sized pieces of cloth that are sewn together according to traditional dimensions.)

He replied that she could and added, "The name of this kind of *kesa* is *funzoe*, which is a *kesa* made of rags. In the early days, monks in training used to wear robes made out of rags. Rags are discarded, unwanted things. These days, the *kesa* is gorgeous. But Shinran wore only a black *kesa* throughout his life. The *kesa* is more important than the cloth it's made from. Anyway, tomorrow you can measure my *gakumon-gesa*."

> The voice you heard
> in the mountains yesterday—
> the echo of something
> that's yet to utter itself in you
> —Namu Amida Butsu.

◆ A *Second Visit to Stone Buddha Mountain*

Patrick, an old friend and writer from California, had come to stay, and each day we all went out together, either to show him somewhere that we had found of interest or to discover with him a place unknown to us. My having been intrigued by Stone Buddha Mountain, and Masako's not having seen it, resulted in our decision to visit one afternoon.

At first it took us some time to find the turnoff from the main road leading past the rice fields to the foot of the path that led up through the forest. We finally located the path and parked the car where we had left it on our previous visit, releasing ourselves from the vehicle's seemingly ever-smaller interior.

We progressed up the track in single file until we came to the spot where the *shimenawa* lay on the ground. At this point, I was in the lead with Masako behind me and Pat bringing up the rear. I had just reached the very large tree around which the narrow path curved, bringing the standing stone into view, and had my left hand spread against the trunk to keep my balance when, looking down so as not to trip over a root, something caught my attention out of the corner of my eye. In a recess at the base of the tree, which I had not previously noticed, I suddenly saw a large snake. Its head was drawn back in preparation to strike. In what became a calm, silent, and suspended time/space of no-movement, all my senses seemed gathered in my eye and focused on its head, tracing the path of its imminent strike to my ankle in a curiously detached way. Then in a sudden return to non-meditative consciousness and environmental rush, I quickly leapt away from the tree, nearly falling in the stream, and called a warning to Masako over my shoulder. Pat came rushing up, and we all stared into the recess, where the tension in the snake's body had relaxed and it was retreating into the darkness of the

tree's interior, allowing us all to pass safely by the tree
and into the arena in front of the stones.

"That was lucky," said Masako, as we rounded the tree.
"It was a *mamushi*. A very poisonous snake."

The snake had had a strange effect, as though we had
been inspected by some authority and given permission
to enter. We joked that it must have been the kami itself
giving us the once over.

After examining the stones, we climbed farther up
above them. There was no path, and it was extremely
steep, necessitating going on hands and knees and haul-
ing oneself up. A few yards farther up there was another
standing stone in direct alignment with the one below it.
It struck me that they were positioned in the same way
that the main altar, where one prays and makes offerings,
and the inner sanctum—the actual dwelling place of the
kami—are placed in the later designs of a Shintō shrine.

Finally we reached the tree-covered summit, and by
descending one side we reconnected with the forestry
track, at the foot of which we had left the car. As we reached
the foot, a farmer's small, white pickup approached and
parked a few yards away just above a rice field.

We wondered if he might have some knowledge of
Stone Buddha Mountain, so we went over and greeted
him, while I was feeling a little apprehensive that we may
have trespassed on what was obviously an important
spiritual center locally. He was very friendly, and when we
explained that we had just visited the stones and asked if
he knew anything about them, he replied, "Ah, that kami
is very important to us farmers. He's a kami that likes to
stay in the dark of the forest. And he doesn't like women."
He laughed. "Once a long time ago, the local lord tried to
take a mare up there, but she got stuck between two trees
and he had to bring her down again. That kami won't even
allow a female horse up there. I can't tell you much about
it, but there's someone in the village who can. He's a

retired school teacher. Sometimes people who are interested in Stone Buddha Mountain visit him." He squatted in the middle of the track and with the aid of a stick sketched in the dry mud a rough map of a nearby village. He drew the main road, a crossroad, a post office, and a house nearly opposite it, which he said was the teacher's house.

We thanked him and set off back to Sora, intending to seek out the school teacher at a later date.

◆ The Hot Spring and Old Man Gonsaku's Hot Dog

While Pat was staying with us, we decided to take him to Mawaki Onsen, the hot spring Mrs. Tani's uncle had been in charge of developing, which overlooks the rice fields, harbor, and village of Mawaki. Once an ancient Jōmon-period (circa 8,000–200 B.C.) settlement, many artifacts, mainly pottery, had been discovered on the site.

There are two main bathhouses, each with its own garden and outdoor baths, so that one can move from the indoors to the outdoors, depending on weather and inclination. The water in these baths is good for treating a variety of ailments. One bathhouse is designed in the form of male genitals and constructed of wood, while the other is designed in the form of female genitals and made from rocks and stones. One week the men bathe in the penis-shaped bathhouse, and the women in the vagina-shaped one. The following week the bathing arrangements are reversed.

On returning to the village after relaxing at the hot spring, Patrick and I in the vagina and Masako in the penis, we found Old Man Gonsaku shelling beans. He was sitting on the ground beside the fire-equipment hut with a piece of wood in one hand and a stump of tree before him, on which he was beating the dried bean plants he had brought from where they had been drying. He was surrounded by little black beans scattered on the ground all around him.

I went over to him and we greeted each other and started up a conversation, as Masako and Pat joined us. While we were talking, I noticed one of the village dogs walking around us, regarding the proceedings with a certain look in its eye. After a few circumambulations, it suddenly came up behind Old Man Gonsaku and without warning leapt on his back with its paws over his shoulders and started to vigorously and enthusiastically "roger" him. Old Man Gonsaku froze with his arm on a downward sweep, and his jaw dropped. He seemed to remain paralyzed in this position for some seconds, while the dog, panting and pumping, had its way with his back. Then, suddenly, time and circumstance caught up with Old Man Gonsaku and with a roar he brought his right hand, holding the piece of wood, back over his head, powerfully hitting the dog square on the nose. It let out a yelp and with the look of a jilted lover fled down the road.

As our laughter simmered down, Old Man Gonsaku looked at us with his eyes wider than I had ever seen them and he roared again. "Aarrrrrgh! If I let him carry on, he might have fallen in love with me."

◆ Our Next-door Neighbor and a Funeral

Yukiko Kamoda was our next-door neighbor. She lived with her husband and her mother-in-law. Her husband, who was already sick when we arrived in the village, died about a year later. And while we very rarely saw him because of his condition, he often expressed his concern for our welfare through Yukiko.

Our kitchen windows opened directly onto the wall of one of her barns and the path between our houses that led to her yard and back door. A lot of our communication with her was done through these windows, and she often passed vegetables or "flowers for Buddha" from her garden up to us there, since the top of her head just reached the sill.

Yukiko seemed, like so many women of the village, to be constantly expressing gratitude. I can hear her voice as I type this, repeating "A*rigatō ne, arigatō ne, arigatō ne,*" after someone had done something for her, or given her a gift, or asked after her health, long after that person had departed down the road, or after Yukiko herself had disappeared back into the interior of her house, I would still hear "A*rigato ne, arigato ne, arigato.*"

Yukiko never wore her teeth. Whether she had lost them or just never owned any, I do not know, but it gave her Japanese, which I found difficult to understand anyway, its own particular enunciation. She had the sweet innocent aura of a child or, perhaps better, an artless being, as the emerging ego of a child can often produce quite the opposite. Her house was virtually unfurnished except for the bare essentials of living, as, like most of the old people, apart from the winter her life was mainly spent out of doors.

Cats were especially attracted to her house, and there were several generations that lived in the spaces beneath the buildings around her yard. One year, Hana (Flower) decided to have her kittens in our barn, and from there they all gained access to the wall and floor spaces of the house. Somehow they managed to get into the space beneath the bath, which was built into the floor. And each time it was filled with hot water, as it was in late autumn, they would congregate there just beneath the bather's bottom, purring and shifting about against the warm base of the tub.

Yukiko's mother-in-law had been badly burned as a young woman by falling into a fire of rice straw in their field one autumn. At the same time, she suffered the

common problem of her spine being so badly curved forward from the waist that she had to support herself on a
stick, even around the house, and only rarely ventured
out with the support of a child's pram.

She had always been under the impression (as they
had no mirror in the house) that her face was very badly
scarred. But after Masako had taken a photograph of her,
she was delighted to find that her face not only looked
unblemished but younger than she had imagined. Yukiko
was delighted with the photograph and told us that she
had been worried that there was no picture of her mother-in-law to place on the altar after she died.

On hot summer evenings, Yukiko's yard became the
focus for many of the old women in the neighborhood,
who would come and sit, gossiping and reminiscing with
her and her mother-in-law. One of these old women was
Old Man Gonsaku's wife, and this meant that it sometimes gave Old Man Gonsaku the excuse to shuffle over
and have a word or two or to make an obscene suggestion, at which gales of laughter or expressions of disgust
would arise, depending on the mood of the day or the
composition of the group or, indeed, the suggestion.

Another member of these evening-backyard soirees
was Mrs. Nakagishi. She lived just a little farther down the
road from Old Man Gonsaku's on the opposite side, and
for months after our arrival completely ignored us as if we
simply did not exist. It was only much later that we
learned that like so many of the old people she literally
could not see us because her eyesight was so bad. She
was in fact a very friendly woman. She was very gaunt and
spare, which made her seem much taller than she actually was, with a rather forbidding scowl written into her
face, perhaps due to her poor eyesight. She held her arms
stiffly back and bent at the elbows like palsied wings, and
when not actually engaged in speech her jaw worked
incessantly, as though the energy of some hitherto unex-

pressed business had left her "chewing over the fat." But when you met her, or watched her in conversation with another, she seemed to be briefly drawn out of some personal darkness, and her expression would change to that of sympathetic engagement.

It was while I was away trying to deepen my knowledge of Japanese that Yukiko's husband died of liver cancer. Rev. Tani had phoned Masako to tell her of his death, and on the eve of the funeral she had joined five of the women from the immediate neighborhood at the house of Mrs. Tabata, who was the daughter of Haru Takiya, "The Woman of Seven Thousand Steps." While the men from these households had the task of arranging the space in the house of the deceased, it was the women's job to prepare rice cakes for the funeral.

By the time Masako arrived, the women were already milling the rice in an old stone hand-mill. After the flour was ground, it was mixed with water and rolled into small balls, which were flattened between the palms of the hands. The rice cakes were then steamed and afterward allowed to cool before being arranged in tiers on the altar, which was formed from Mr. Kamoda's coffin covered in a white cloth and decorated with flowers, a photograph of Mr. Kamoda, and a wooden funerary tablet (*ihai*) bearing his posthumous Buddhist name. In front of this altar was a basket filled with paper flowers, fruit, and various gifts of food and saké from relatives. The rice cakes were distributed among the mourners after the funeral to be eaten as a prevention against illness.

At seven o'clock that evening, Masako went next-door to Yukiko's house with a small gift of money and sat through the hour's chanting by Rev. Tani and another Shingon priest. During the chanting, a tray bearing incense and a burner was passed between the mourners so they could offer incense.

On the afternoon of the following day, the day of the

funeral, the men representing the households involved in the funeral preparations were invited to the house of an eighty-year-old neighbor who lived on the road at the back of our house. As I was absent, Masako was asked to represent our household. There they were served on individual red-lacquer tables and tableware and ate red-bean rice (usually eaten in Japan at celebrations, but traditionally at funerals in Sora), soup, cooked vegetables, and noodles with saké to drink. During this time, Yukiko and the rest of the mourners were attending the cremation of her husband's body, after which she returned to her house with his ashes in a white ceramic funerary urn.

For forty-nine days after the funeral, Yukiko and her mother-in-law were restricted to a vegetarian diet, while the priest would visit at intervals to chant before the ashes of her husband to ensure a beneficial rebirth. At the end of this period, the ashes were placed in the family grave, and she carried all the funeral decorations in her barrow and dumped them over the side of the quay into the sea.

One day Yukiko came into our *genkan* to confirm that we did not possess a television. It seemed that something had happened that she needed to tell us about. "Whenever the box people make a noise, something bad has happened. I don't like the box, but I watch it a lot. When we didn't have a box, we didn't know what was going on in the world, so we didn't need to worry so much. But these days the box makes a lot of noise, and I have more worries.

"Although the box is shouting out a warning, I can't understand it very well because I'm an idiot. But they said a big typhoon is coming to our area, so you have to be careful. I have to tell you this, because you haven't got a box."

In any event, we only experienced the rim of the storm.

The sky turned a strange color as though it had been taken ill and might vomit undigested satellites and the odd plane later in the day, and the air suddenly became like living downwind from a volcano. But apart from that, the demons were dancing elsewhere.

> *Time hangs heavy*
> *on the sleeve of a cloud.*
> *Brings the flowers*
> *come crashing down.*
> *Works the lips*
> *to call the names*
> *of those*
> *already gone.*

◆ A Weaver's Tale

In the past each house owned a handloom, but in recent years most have disappeared, leaving only the echo of their shuttles in the saying "If you can't weave well, you can't marry." But thirty years ago, a master weaver, Ueshima Yozan, the thirteenth generation of a famous family of weavers, visited Noto from Kyoto. In the weaving shops in Kyoto at that time, there had been a changeover from hand-weaving to electrically operated looms—a move he deplored. He was so impressed by the hands of the women farmers he met in Noto that he decided to reintroduce them to weaving on handlooms and set up several groups of weavers in the villages. One of these groups was made up of six of the women in Sora, who took over one of the empty houses and converted it into a weaving workshop.

We were sitting talking with one of the weavers, Mrs. Kawasaki, over a cup of tea in the workshop one day when she said, "Before we got the looms, our husbands went to the big cities to work on building sites, road construction, and in factories, while we had to look after the old parents and the children and work in the rice fields. In the winter, we wanted to get some small job to earn money, but it was impossible to leave home. One day we were told about this weaving job. In our grandmothers' generation all women could weave. They wove all the kimonos for their families. But we weren't taught how to do it. So when we heard of someone who would teach us, six of us decided to take this job. We were very nervous. At first I couldn't sleep at night. And we had to start using hand cream because our hands were so rough from farming!" She flashed her gold teeth in a laugh.

She went on to describe how expensive it was having to buy clothes, and I said that in the West we do not mind wearing second-hand clothes and, in fact, where once it had been fashionable among young people to do so, now in the recession it had become a necessity for a lot of people. She expressed surprise, since it was not some-thing generally practiced among her generation, and then suddenly became thoughtful for a minute. "It's said that if you wear something that belonged to your dead mother you can avoid getting sick. I suddenly remembered this once when I was sick in bed and I put on my mother's vest. I immediately felt better. It was very strange."

I was about to mention the obvious psychological rea-son, when I began to think of how many in the West derived little or no comfort from their living mothers, let alone from their dead mother's clothes. Instead I told her how I once bought a second-hand old man's overcoat and every time I put it on my whole body ached. I assumed the original owner must have suffered from arthritis or something.

She laughed and went on, "These days our life is real-ly easy." I was just wondering, watching their lives, how they could possibly be much harder, when she began to elaborate. "When I was young and you got married, you had to live with your in-laws, and you only got to visit your parents twice a year, even if they only lived in the next village. In this area we called visiting our parents *sendaku*, 'a holiday for the daughter-in-law to visit her parents.' What it really meant was a working holiday! We had to put all the family's dirty kimonos and whatever else needed patching or repairing into a huge wrapping cloth and carry this bundle on our backs to our parents' village.

"We usually stayed with our parents for two weeks. During this time, we had to unstitch each kimono in order to wash it and then sew it up again. As you know, you can't wash a kimono as it is. We also had to repair and patch the kimonos, as well as all the other things. We couldn't do these at our in-law's house because we had no time—it was taken up with farming, looking after the children, and housework.

"Anyway, by the time I got back to my in-laws, everything was clean and mended. I also brought back new cotton kimonos, which we wore for the spring planting with the sleeves tucked up and tied with a red cord. These days no one bothers with such things anymore. But when I was young, it was important to wear certain types of kimonos for different kinds of jobs, so that when I was at my parents' house I had to make this kind of working kimono as well. Can you imagine parents having to accept their daughters back home with all that work?

"When I got married, my parents bought me all the kimonos I would need throughout my life. This was common. We weren't to spend any money on ourselves, especially while our husband's parents were alive. We couldn't be seen buying anything for ourselves, as good evidence to the rest of the village that we weren't spending any of our husband's family's money.

"These days our life is very different. In our young days it wasn't easy at all. But I think I'm lucky. Now I'm enjoying farming and weaving as well."

◆ Old Man Gonsaku and the Red Paint

The summer of 1994 was so relentlessly hot and dry that
farmers spent the whole day from 4:30 A.M. carting water
to their rice fields in tanks and any receptacle available.
Even so, more than half of the rice crop in the area of Sora
and the surrounding villages was destroyed. The old people even began to collapse and die in the heat as they
worked in their fields. The ambulance came to the village
several times, and on each occasion we would all trace
the sound of its siren around the maps of the area in our
imaginations to see where it was going. Once it entered
the village people dropped whatever they were doing and
left their houses, following it down the street to see
whose house it would stop at. When anyone was sick,
everyone was involved, because they were either directly
or indirectly related or at least had known that person
since childhood.

It was on one such occasion when an ambulance had
been heard in the district that, talking to Old Man
Gonsaku in the road outside his house, he told us how
once he had been taken by ambulance to the hospital in
Anamizu.

"One day, I went to Anamizu by bicycle for shopping. At
that time, we already had the railway stations in Kabuto
and near Kanami, but I didn't use the train because it
was too expensive. I bought a can of red paint in the town
and drank some saké at a saké shop. On my way home,
I couldn't find my way down the hill into the village, so I
stopped my bicycle and as I turned around to see where
I was, I lost my balance and fell over. It was just in front
of Kabuto Primary School. The paint can was thrown out
of the basket, the lid came off, and I got covered in red
paint, all over my head and face and shoulders. It was a
special paint for protecting boats and didn't have any
smell." He started to giggle.

"Just after I fell, the school teacher's wife came over the
hill in her car. When she saw me in the road, she thought

I was seriously injured and covered in blood. She phoned for an ambulance. You know the small shop by the school? She ran in there and used their phone.

"When she came back out, I told her I was all right and that the red stuff was only paint, but she wouldn't believe me. She just believed I was seriously injured and covered in blood. I probably couldn't speak properly, because, you know, I'd been drinking saké in Anamizu." He giggled again.

"Anyway, an ambulance came, and again I said I was all right, but they didn't believe me either and they put me in the ambulance. That teacher's wife also phoned my *babā* and told her I was seriously injured. So seriously, she said, that the blood had forgotten to stop." He broke off and started another wobble of giggles.

"On the way to the hospital, the ambulance men began to think it was a bit strange and wondered if I really was injured. But they still had to take me to the hospital. Anyway, as I told you, the paint didn't smell, you know. If it smelled like ordinary paint, they wouldn't have needed to make such a fuss.

"When the doctor examined me, he said, 'There's nothing wrong with you. You can go home.' I told him, 'I'm fine. But you brought me here, you should take me home. I can't afford it.' Then the doctor sent me home by taxi.

"Since then, the nurses have handed down this story over the years. Even today, everybody in the hospital knows me. You know, I told them I was all right."

He was off giggling again and supporting his body against a wall of his house. Then he walked down the side of the house and returned with a hoe and went off in the direction of his vegetable garden.

◆ Night Call

In the early hours of August 16, 1994, we were awakened at 3:00 A.M. by the telephone. Masako had reached the phone before me, as I staggered up from the futon into the dense, humid and heat-thick dark of the house, trying to plumb my mind for anyone who could be calling at this hour. Very quickly, as my consciousness reassembled itself, I sensed some indefinable pool of anxiety, which immediately congealed as Masako called out that it was for me.

I took hold of the handset. A voice on the other end said, "It's John." There was a pause and my mind scanned a few of the several Johns I know and have known in the past. Then, "Your brother. It's Dad. I'm afraid I've got some terrible news. Dad died this afternoon."

In the space in which comprehension seemed to be on hold, he went on to explain that our mother had called Dad in for tea from the garden, where he had been working, and that when he did not appear immediately, she had started eating, expecting him at any moment. When he failed to arrive, she had gone to look for him, but being unable to find him anywhere in the garden, she had gone to a neighbor, a retired Irish diplomat, who made a cursive search of the village. On failing to locate him, he had gone back into the garden and happened to look in a potting shed, where he found my father dead on the floor.

There was a momentary confluence of the silences in the house, the village, and the peninsula beyond with the silence in the place at the other end of the phone. Then this collective silence was broken, with an accompanying spatial separation between the handset, my ear, and the voice of my brother thousands of kilometers away, by a sob in his throat.

The next day I made immediate arrangements for a flight to Britain. The last time we had been in Japan, it had been Masako's father who had died.

My father had been a stranger to me and me to him, due to his absence for long periods during my earliest years because of the war, and later, his being posted to India. He had been a fighter pilot in the Battle of

Britain—'one of the few'—and paradoxically, in my mind, it was at this time, while in the constant company of death, that he appears to have been imbued with a life-affirming energy which seemed to have deserted him on his return from India. Even his physical presence, on a psychological and emotional level, was experienced by me, at the time, as an absence. After the war, when his remaining years in the air force were spent "flying a desk" at the Ministry of Defense, his life became more and more lived by the book. So insurance-safe did it become that it acquired the risk-free security of a coffin—a nonliving way to escape the risk of life which, in the conventional drawing rooms of the middle class, supported a mirage of living. Behind my father's compulsive patterns for doing everything "properly" was a drift of unresolved darkness; a life whose tight sail was filled by an indefinable and relentless fear, which totally excluded me and blew me into an increasing centrifuge of anxiety. Perhaps in mimicry of his own fear or in my fear of him, I had caught the stench from an invisible war-wound.

Two years before his death, I had stayed for two days with my parents and without Masako for the first time in many years. During this time my father and I had had the only row we had ever had, in fact the only true communication in our lives, and I confronted him with all the things that I had held in my body since I was a baby and he returned from India. It was an occasion when, for the second time, he cast me out of the family "forever." On reaching home, I had written him a long letter, restating a lot of what I had said in anger and setting the whole situation as I experienced it in as clear and lucid prose as I could manage.

For three months I heard nothing. Then one day I received a friendly four-page letter from him. I had never received a letter from him in my life. Not even as a child away at boarding school. A new and tentative relationship was beginning in which he began to talk about his own personal problems. He had phoned us in Japan and talked for half an hour, never having phoned me in his life before, the week before he died.

Ironically, since he quite rightly left everything to my mother, what I did receive from my father, who was never able to give me any of his time during his life, was an eighteenth-century bracket clock, three fob watches, and his service watch.

After I had returned to Japan, I heard from my mother that my brother had arranged for his ashes to be dropped from a World War II bomber.

◆ Old Wounds

After my father's funeral, I had to visit a couple living near my parent's house, the husband of which had also been in the air force. I was returning a large dish the wife had lent my mother for the reception following the funeral.

The front door was answered by the wife, who was wearing a dressing-gown and held a duster in her hand, with which she nervously polished the front-door knob for the duration of our short conversation. I thanked her for the loan of the dish, and she asked how my mother was. She then called to her husband, who appeared hesitantly, also in a dressing-gown, in the back shadows of the sitting room. In attempting to explain his ethereal presence, as if he were only a portrait of her husband hanging back in the dark, she said, "It's difficult for him, you know. You see, he was a prisoner."

Stupidly, the meaning she was trying to communicate to me did not register until she had closed the door and I was walking away down the garden path. The only flowers that were present at the crematorium—my mother having expressed the wish, unknown to me, that donations should be made to charity in lieu of such—were from Masako's family and two or three Japanese friends of ours. The sight of these flowers with their Japanese messages had obviously sadly upset him.

As I write this, it is the fiftieth anniversary of JV Day, and the media is filled with the complicated passions and opinions concerning the treatment of allied prisoners of war by the Japanese on the one side, and the horrors of the atomic bombs on Hiroshima and Nagasaki on the other. There are the confused attempts by the Japanese government to apologize for the inhumanities committed during the war, and the West's demand that these be made clear as an admission of guilt and remorse by the Japanese people, coupled with America's equally confused rationalizations, lies, and justifications for dropping the bombs.

Whilst in no way excusing or dismissing the inhuman behavior of Japanese, or any other troops during the Second World War, one has to ask when the British, including whatever colonial nationality we might also have been known by, ever apologized to the Native Americans, the so-called Aborigines, the Maoris (who were recently received an official apology, insufficiently and far too late), the African peoples (including those we now call by the names of other islands and countries), the Irish, and so on. The Tasmanians, for example, we cannot apologize to—we simply wiped them out! Whenever I see the West on its moral high horse, I cannot see its legs, because it simply hasn't a leg to stand on; nor its mouth, because *it* can't talk; nor its eyes, because it's blind to itself; nor its nose, because it can't smell the stench of its own shit! All I see of the West's moral high horse is a bloody great arse!

Somehow the wounds still carried by this man seemed to become part of the tragedy of my father's death, slamming the lid on any possibility of an understanding between us by making me aware that the past war between my own country and that of a country whose people and past culture I love—the native land of my wife—still keeps a door locked within the hearts of some people.

This experience also revived a memory of traveling in a taxi through Tokyo and getting into a conversation with the driver, who owned the cab and was a man in his seventies, about the same age as my father. After discussing various common topics, he suddenly started to describe how he had been a pilot during the war in the Pacific and that every year the surviving members of his squadron hold a reunion. He told us about a collection of journals he had, which had been published by his squadron and, recounted their exploits during the war. He said he no longer wanted them in his house, that they made him tired, and he was thinking of burning them. Then half turning in his seat, he said he suddenly had the feeling that he wanted to give them to me. Would I mind if he posted them to me? I told him I would be very interested in receiving them and gave him our address. A week later, a box arrived containing thirty or forty volumes of his squadron's personal records, including his own.

I did not know it at the time, but I was to learn more about the wartime experiences of this pilot, who was a stranger to me, than those of my own father, a pilot, who was also a stranger to me.

◆ Genetic Nightmare

After making sure that the arrangements for my mother's immediate future were in order and before returning to Japan, I traveled down to Cornwall to visit an old friend called Heathcote, who is talented in a number of fields and whom I had known and admired for some twenty-five years. At the time, he was staying on a farm of an old school friend of his while using the fourteenth-century chapel attached to the main house as a painting studio.

There were two other house guests at the time—a couple visiting from America. The husband was English but had been living and working in the States for a number of years. On coming into the room, he introduced himself to me as ". . . a world authority on genetics." To this day I cannot remember his name, since it was entirely blown away by this inflated presumption.

Over dinner, the conversation was light and casual. But after dinner, in the sitting room in front of a log fire, enjoying a glass of single malt, the geneticist began to speak of his work. As he talked, I began to acquire the cold suspicion that it involved the appalling notion of genetic real estate—the jumping of claims on the discovery of certain genes and the patenting of them, so that anyone wishing to use them for research has to pay a royalty to whomever "discovered" them!

When I inquired if this was part of the nature of his work, he seemed to physically levitate momentarily off the sofa, as though a powerful charge had passed between the poles of his body, and explained that that was exactly his domain. Then with a complacent smile he asserted, "Soon we're going to be able to cure every sickness."

As I was also a house guest, and not wishing to create an embarrassing situation for my host, particularly since the geneticist was a paying guest, I sat uncomfortably on my reaction. Something of its import must have been transmitted on a fart of pheromones, however, because he suddenly emptied his glass and, excusing himself, went up to bed.

On my way up to bed, I thought to myself, "Isn't that the greatest sickness of all? And isn't it precisely just this kind of arrogant scientific-consumer-materialism that has resulted in terrestrial AIDS—the hole in the ozone layer, the Earth's immune system—which has so strangely coincided with the appearance of AIDS in human beings?" I prayed that he would soon recover from his own sickness.

That night my dreams were trampled by nightmares released from the stables of some genetic hell, bolting like steeds of evil lightning down the aisles of baby-of-your-choice boutiques—the sound of the jackboots of the cloned armies of a moonless, skyless night, bearing armfuls of gene catalogues scripted by a Hollywood-based totalitarian regime, and evil empires gagging on their own genicidal shadows.

By morning I was longing for the smells of Sora's main street!

◆ Techno-Toilet

A great deal of technology is an externalization or extension of abilities, often forgotten or seldom realized, which we possess as human beings. Most of the so-called convenience technologies we have developed, however, are in fact inconvenient in a deep and fundamental way to both body and mind and detrimental to the human spirit. One obvious example is in the way certain technologies kill our capacity for intuition, for the natural skills of timing and measuring, and for simply using our own bodies.

I discovered one of the most extreme and trivial forms of convenience technology actually in a "convenience"—a toilet in a guest house attached to a Buddhist temple! I had just finished my business and, declining the conveniences indicated on the console beside the electrically heated seat on which I sat—that is, warm water sprayed up the anus followed by zephyrs of warm air (I tried that particular convenience once and due to some faulty thermostat departed hurriedly with a burned scrotum)—I availed myself of paper.

The real problem came when I turned to flush the thing. I first visually searched the surface of the plum-colored, pod-shaped tank in vain. I then examined it with my hands, like a doctor searching for swollen glands. I pushed, prodded, and passed my hands over every suggestion of a lug, or imagined button, indentation, or infrared beam, and every area of change of color to no avail. Turning toward the door, my eyes lit on a remote-control console sitting in a plastic holster on the wall. I suspected that this must somehow relate to the undiscovered flushing function. I removed it from the holster and surveyed the *kanji* (Chinese characters) on its buttons, only recognizing two of them, neither of which related to the business of flushing. I decided against a hit-and-miss method lest I trigger some irreversible function or find myself teleported into a toilet in some other time zone.

Shame-faced, but in fact feeling an emotion quite different from shame, I carried the gadget before me, like some kind of electronic Rosetta Stone, into the kitchen where the household was gathered to inquire as to which button to press. As the button was pointed out to me, my eyes lost focus on the remote control and focused instead on my feet directly below it. They were still clad in the plastic slippers emblazoned in English with the word "Toilet," as they stood on the immaculate kitchen floor! I had failed to change out of the toilet slippers and into the house slippers, which I should then have exchanged for the kitchen slippers, with the subsequent necessity for reversing this procedure on my journey back. I returned hastily to the toilet and, before I was even through the door, found myself aiming the gadget at the plastic tank, imagining I was flushing the whole contraption into a far distant galaxy!

◆ Winter

I woke in the night with a dog barking at the far end of the village. As I lay there I realized that it could be any dog, in any place, in any country of the world. I had woken in New York, in Glasgow, in Thailand, in Sri Lanka, in Cornwall, in California, in Tokyo, on Arran, in Melbourne, in London to the same dog barking. It was as though I carried this night with this barking dog around in my body someplace, or that the same dog shadowed me, turning up wherever I went—a guide dog in the blindness of my night. I lay listening to it, and it was as familiar to me as my own breathing in the dark, through a nose so sensitive to subtle smell that it is a faculty people often relate with a dog's nose.

Slowly, the barking reached back into the country of my dreams, and when I next awoke, the room was so suffused with a familiar light and quality of silence that when I got up and went to the window I was not surprised to find that snow had fallen.

Going outside, the village had been edited down to its most prominent features—poles, roofs, the temple belfry, the change of plane and surface at the waterfront and the moored boats, the bristle-brindled flatness of the rice fields surrounded by the white, lumpy hills, and from the shoreline the blank infinity of sea-sky.

When you first go outside into the snow the air has that almost interior warmth and silence of a room. Whereas hot sun releases and intensifies all smells in a way that gives the most unexpected object its own scent, its olfactory charge, snow is an editor of smells. In snow, in the village, the smell of kerosene becomes illuminated and periodic, like commencing a repeated sentence in the Book of Sora. Behind it, or beneath it, sometimes there is the thin acridity of urine. The only time this changes is when baths are fired and the falling flakes become infused with the rising, resinous perfume of wood smoke. The rest is white smell—olfactory white-out. It must be like another kind of darkness to a dog.

In the winter cold the herons pull their necks so far

down into their bodies that their bills appear at unexpected places, making it look as though each has been shot with an arrow. And the plaintive cries of kites posted on electricity poles all over the village seem to quaver palpably like thin miseries across the roofs. Days and nights share the same rhythm of snow and thaw, snow and thaw, behind a constant curtain of water running off gutterless roofs or roofs where gutters have been blocked for years. This is punctuated by the regular slide-thud of small avalanches crashing from the tiles.

In a traditional Japanese farmhouse in the winter, sources of heating are very localized, and it is so cold moving about that you often wear a hat and always thermal underwear. You tend to stay in. It is a time for gossip and stories, saké, Japanese chess (*shōgi* and *go*) and hot soup and noodles, and bits of paper in cracks to foil the drafts.

> *Last summer*
> I *heard rumor of it,*
> *and now it's here—*
> *snow on the wind-face*
> *of the electricity pole.*

◆ New Year's Party

Masako had been invited to the women's New Year's party in the village hall. This communal place, for the duration of the party, was declared out of bounds to the menfolk.

After the party, Masako told me that one old woman had gotten up and danced while another sang. The old woman who danced wore a *tenugui* (small hand towel) from her waist like a loincloth, while beneath it hung a penis fashioned from a second rolled-up *tenugui*. She danced the part of a man fishing in a river with a scoop-shaped basket, placing the fish he caught in a bag at his waist. Now and again "he" would lift his loincloth and shake his penis at the women.

◆ Mr. Morishita's Treasure

On the afternoon of New Year's Day there was a voice in the *genkan*, and I heard Masako answer and then call to me up the stairs where I was in my workroom. I went downstairs to find a young couple who addressed me in perfect English. The man introduced himself as Max Nakajima and explained over tea that he had been born in the village but since university he had lived in America and was now living in Nagano, where he was the assistant manager in the export department of a plastics firm.

During our conversation he asked me what we were doing in Sora, and I explained that I was thinking about writing a book about the village. On hearing about the kinds of things that interested me, he proceeded to tell me a story.

"When my mother was pregnant with my elder brother and in labor, a very old great-aunt of mine, who was a healer, gave my mother a piece of paper with the *nembutsu* (a form of the name of Amida Buddha) written on it to protect her. She was directed to screw the piece of paper into a tight ball and swallow it with a glass of water, like a pill. When my brother was born, they noticed that he had one hand tightly closed into a fist, and upon opening his fingers, they found he was holding the piece of paper with the *nembutsu* written on it."

From a physiological point of view this of course makes no sense. But we later asked Max's mother about the story. At first she was embarrassed that we had been told about it. Then she said "Yes, it's true. But whenever I told anyone about it, they just thought I was stupid or had made it up. So I stopped telling anyone anymore."

Now one might expect that anyone with such an apparently auspicious birth would be destined to become either a great monk or a healer or something. In fact, while being described as a very upright and honest young man, he works in a local tax office!

After seeing my obvious interest in the story, Max suggested that he bring his uncle, who lived about a mile from the village on the high ground above it, to visit and tell some of his stories. We arranged for him to come to tea with his uncle the following day.

Max's uncle was a small, delicate-boned man with a soft feminine manner, like many of the men of Sora. He introduced himself in the *genkan* as Mr. Morishita, and we showed him and Max through to the kitchen where they sat while Masako and I prepared the tea things.

I had heard from Max that his uncle, like many of the villagers, wrote haiku, and while I was arranging some food on plates I asked him about it.

"In Anamizu there are about thirty haiku lovers. I'm one of them, and I've been a member of the haiku group for eight years. There's also a small group in Kabuto, which I started. Mr. Tabata, Mr. Asai, and Mr. Kawasaki, all from Sora, started writing haiku in the Kabuto group. Now they all belong to the Anamizu group. They're excellent."

"Mrs. Haru Takiya and Mr. Muroki also write haiku, don't they?" Masako asked, pouring hot water into a teapot.

"Yes, all of these people joined the group some years ago when I started it and was head of it. Now I've passed it on to Mr. Muroki. The haiku group in Anamizu is like the headquarters of all the smaller groups in the villages around the town."

Tea was prepared and as she lifted one of the trays Masako turned to Mr. Morishita and asked, "Which room would you be comfortable in? If you prefer tatami we can go upstairs to the workroom, which is already warm."

"I'm fine anywhere," he replied, taking up a *tenugui* from the table where he had left it.

We all went upstairs to the workroom where the stove had been on most of the day. We arranged ourselves around the table beside my desk, Mr. Morishita choosing to sit with his back to the window, through which I noticed large flakes of snow beginning to fall.

As tea was being poured, Mr. Morishita wiped his nose thoughtfully on his *tenugui* and continued on the subject of haiku. "Since my daughter and her husband came back to Sora to live with us it has become rather difficult to attend haiku meetings, because they don't like for me to go out. My wife is a really talented haiku poet. Before they came back she wrote haiku with me, but now she's stopped completely. The reason why they are against me being a member of the haiku group is that the others in the group, except for the two or three from Sora and Kabuto, are intelligent people. They used to be school teachers, one was the head of the local post office, and so on. They are all rich pensioners. My daughter and her husband think that we are only simple farmers from Sora and Kabuto."

Max was looking a little uncomfortable. "In a word," he said in English, "it's due to the family's lack of under-standing. . . ." He looked as though he was about to add something, but for whatever reason decided not to.

In an effort to counterbalance the weight Mr. Morishita obviously felt burdened with, we explained to him how much we were learning from people in the village and tried to describe the value we saw in their way of life and how living in harmony and accord with the cycles of nature was a very precious wisdom. "What is sometimes thought of as intelligence and learning is often a kind of great stupidity . . ." I started to say, when he interrupted.

"Well, we can't be true farmers if we're calculating. If we're not living calmly and leaving everything to Nature, we can't be farmers. Writing haiku and poems and not thinking too seriously, this is the way," he said, and as he wiped his nose a heron flew past the window behind him, trailing its empty legs through the falling snow. "If you can't reach this point, you'll be miserable. Lots of people complain that farming is unprofitable, but if we can switch our ideas about the way we work, from profitability to one of the Buddha's will, farming can be such a lovely job.

"Thinking of Ryōkan or Bashō, if we are only working for money, we will never be like them. From today's point of view, they might be seen as lazy in a sense, because they didn't work. But after their leisurely life their names remain in history. Hundreds of years later we still admire them. This might be the power of culture. If we can think of our life more flexibly and spend a little more time reading and writing, the country is really a good place to live. But if we feel that it's a disadvantage to live in the country, then we can't stay here. Most of us don't realize how lucky we are to live in the country. For example, my wife stopped writing haiku under the influence of our son-in-law who is a money-minded man," he laughed. "She hesitates to do anything that goes against his ideas because he is the heir.

"On the whole, the cultural standard around here is not high. In this environment, farmers who write haiku are thought to be rather peculiar by some people. This doesn't make her feel free enough to write haiku, which means she keeps her desire to herself. This is my wife's situation. Compared to me she is much more gifted. I think that if both of us can learn more about writing haiku together it will be the best way for us to live. But these days she's given it up completely. She just says, 'It's not for farmers.' Though the people in Anamizu said to me 'You're lucky, you're living in the best environment.' Even so, my family never understands. . . ." His words evaporated into thoughts and he stared abstractedly at the table in front of him. The snow beyond his shoulder had turned powdery and dry, as if someone in the sky was sawing up a cloud for fuel to rekindle the sun, which had been dead for some days.

It felt as though he had been holding onto his disappointment for a long time and briefly needed a rest after its airing. Masako offered him a biscuit, and he lifted his cup for the first time since it had been filled, with the customary, polite "*Itadakimasu*," before he drank from it.

He drank his tea quietly for a few minutes while we talked among ourselves about one thing or another, then on a little prompting from Max he began again.

"My father's eldest sister died at eighty-five or -six. The day she died her grandson was working with me, and after work he went back home. When he entered the house his grandmother was waiting there for him. As soon as she saw he was home she went into her room and she died there. What I mean is that she knew she was going to die and she decided exactly when. Her sect was the Shingon sect, so she had to put on white *tekkō* [formal covering for the back of the hands] and white *kyahan* [cloth gaiters], which are the clothes for the last journey. She died by herself in her room.

"When I was young, she was rather unusual. She wasn't one of those ordinary farmer's wives that you see around. She prayed *Namu Daishi Henjō Kongō* because she belonged to the Shingon sect, and she healed sick people. Healing seemed to be her pleasure. She was such a strange aunt. She had many followers. People even visited her from the end of the peninsula. She not only healed people, she could also tell if it was going to be a bumper year for fishing and farming. Her readings came true; that's why she had a lot of followers. She had no desire for money at all, so she never accepted payment for her healings or for her readings. All I can remember is that she made her patients drink water. She went to her own family's house to get water from the well, which she put into a cup with a little powdered incense and a piece of paper with *Namu Daishi Henjō Kongō* written on it. I'm not sure where she got these pieces of paper, maybe from Mount Kōya [location of the head temple of the Shingon sect]. She would give this to sick people who had been given up on by the doctors. Very often these people stayed in her house, I remember.

"One old man from Kabuto who used to be the head of an old people's group was healed by this old woman. I remember he visited her often. I think he suffered from TB. Anyway, those who had been given up on by their doctors came to her for treatment and they recovered. In fact, some of them are still alive and in good health today, though of course they're very old now."

He finished the remains of his tea, and Masako poured him a second cup. A kite on a long glide passed the window and flew over the roof. It had stopped snowing and the light outside had developed a purple hue. "She lived such a strange life," he continued, almost directly upon the upward movement of his Adam's apple after swallowing a sip of the fresh tea. "Thinking of her life now, it couldn't have been easy for her family, especially financially. People usually understood that healing was her hobby.

"She had no children so she decided to adopt my elder sister and a son, from a relation in Sora. Her adopted son worked for a salvage company and earned lots of money. He used to send her money, but whenever she received money from him she wouldn't keep it. She donated it all to the temple, so when her adopted son came home he found none of the money he was expecting. She had donated it all. She lived this way to the end of her life. She was a mysterious kind of woman and I think she lived an unusual life."

There was silence for a while, as he crunched on a piece of biscuit, almost impatiently, as though his real hunger lay in his need to talk and eating the biscuit was a formality that merely interrupted satisfying the greater appetite. "At present, Japan has developed into a materialistic civilization, and our minds are getting poorer. In reflecting on the present condition of our life, I began to think of the old woman's life and how we can learn something from her way of living. As I just told you, she donated all her money to the temple whenever she received it. Once I had an argument with her. I said, 'I can't understand you at all!' But she didn't take me seriously. What an old woman!

"I don't know how I should describe her, but I think she had some kind of psychic or special power. She wasn't rich and she never troubled others in terms of money. It's good to keep a balance between finances and our minds. We should try to avoid extremes.

"My family might get angry if they hear what I'm telling you, but I'm not a hard worker. I'm a farmer, but if someone asks what my real job is I really don't know how to answer. My father was a carpenter, so when I came back from the war I did some work with him. During the war I was an orderly in a field hospital, but that was in name only. I actually worked as a carpenter, building temporary hospital buildings whenever we moved. We were in China, so I worked with Chinese carpenters."

He wiped his nose on his *tenugui*, and I noticed that the purple behind him had deepened and that I could see Max's face apparently staring out of the Kitayama's wall on the opposite bank of the river. Then he removed the *tenugui* from his nose and said, "There are many stories in the Noto Peninsula, which I think is a very romantic place. And the remains of the Ainu [the indigenous peoples of Japan] are on Noto Island.

"I moved out of the village and went up the hill behind the temple in 1958. At that time the whole area was forest, and when we were working there clearing the ground, we found lots of arrowheads. These days even ordinary people are talking about this and that in archaeology, but in those days we didn't know anything. Even so, we thought that those stones were strange and unusual.

"One day I brought some of them to the town museum, where I saw some similar types of stones. But before I could ask them any details about the stones, one of my old friends who I hadn't seen for a long time appeared and was so delighted to see me that he invited me for a cup of tea. I totally forgot why I had come into town," he laughed. "Anyway, I've still kept those arrowheads at home."

"Do you think they might be from the Jōmon period?" I asked, looking at the vascular map on the back of his hand as he placed his fingers around his cup.

"Maybe. Or perhaps they could have been made by the Ainu people." He held his head to one side, looking down at the table, considering it. "I think when we are young we tend to deny the spiritual world or mysterious things, but now as I get older I begin to think that the spiritual things are part of our life.

"Today my nephew called on me and said he thought I should see you because I'm interested in psychic, spiritual, and religious things. The elder brother of this boy," he pointed at Max, "who works in the Wajima tax office . . . is a strange man. He is young and very serious, which means he is probably an ideal tax man." He looked around the table at us, and laughed. "Some years ago he visited me and said, 'Uncle, I've brought a book for you.' It was a book on Buddhism."

I wondered why he had not told us the story about Max's brother's birth, but decided that either he knew Max had already told us or he was protecting his sister from any embarassing questions. But now he began, haltingly and with great preamble, to tell a story that really interested me, and one which I still wish to return to Japan to follow up.

"In my house, Shinran's . . . I still can't decide what I

should do . . . how I should understand. . . . The reason why I decided to join the haiku group is this . . . Shinran's . . . . The head of the group in Anamizu is an eighty-five-year-old priest of the Jōdo Shinshū [True Pure Land Sect]. I learned about him from the local newspaper and became interested in him. That's why I decided to join the group. We had haiku gatherings at his house three times, but I never told him what I really wanted to talk to him about.

"Strangely enough, my wife has a very old photograph of herself with a small boy in her arms, which was taken before she was married to me. A traveler who was staying in a guest house in Kabuto visited us, with the same photograph as my wife's. According to the traveler, he had shown the photograph to the owner of the guest house and asked him if he knew the young woman in it. Immediately the owner of the guest house said, 'Ah, it's Morishita's wife.' So the traveler came to visit us. As he introduced himself and handed me his card, he also showed me the photograph and said that the small boy in it was himself.

"When my wife was young, she used to work for a grand family in Matto, and the man's father worked for a company owned by the family. The photograph was taken when his father took him to his office. He knew the young woman in the photograph came from somewhere in Noto, and during the last few years he had had many opportunities to come to Noto because of his job. He said he was working at the site of the Jōmon remains at Mawaki and that whenever he came to Noto he looked for someone who might know the young woman in the photograph. It turned out that he was in charge of the archaeological site at Mawaki.

"While he was staying with us, it was my wife rather than me who said to him, 'Your work is concerned with ancient things, isn't it? We have something very old. Would you mind having a look at it?' And he said 'By all means.' What she described as 'something very old' is something by Shinran.

"When she showed it to him he said, 'This is very unusual. From a historical point of view this kind of thing shouldn't be in Noto.' Then he said that when he went back to his office, he would talk about it with his chief. And sometime later, his chief, himself, and another person came to visit us and asked if I would lend it to them. As a matter of fact, they brought all sorts of things with which to wrap Shinran's object. But at that time I couldn't lend it to them, so I said 'No.' To me they were asking if they could borrow my family treasure, so I hesitated a bit. That's why I refused.

"Then they said, 'That's quite understandable. In that case, would you bring it with you to the prefectural office? We want to show it to someone.' I thought that that would be all right and agreed.

"My son-in-law and I took it by car to Kanazawa where we were met by one of my nephews, and the three of us went to the prefectural office. Tatsusaburō Hayashiya, who had been director of the Kyoto National Museum of Art, was the supervisor of the Prefectural Art Museum of Ishikawa at the time. This man was the expert that they wanted to show it to, but he was a specialist in things that were dug up from the ground. What I have is a piece of paper with something written on it. Consequently, they intended to show the piece of paper to Mr. Hayashiya first and then ask him to introduce us to an expert in the field.

"When we met him, he was accompanied by a woman who was an expert on reading ancient documents, so I showed them the four items I had brought with me, including Shinran's own calligraphy, a written statement by Rennyo authenticating Shinran's calligraphy, and another statement by a man from Higashi Honganji temple in Kyoto who, I learned from them, had been a distinguished priest and scholar.

"There was one more thing I had brought with me. It was a small book for collecting the seals of temples while making a pilgrimage. In this book there's a name and address—Tosuke, Sora Village, Country of Noto—and more than twenty temple seals, showing that the man Tosuke had visited them. It is dated Ansei 3 (1856). I think this man is my ancestor. My head family is Takase in the village, and several generations ago, my family was established as a branch family of Takase; therefore, Tosuke might be a man who set himself up in a new family. Our house is still registered as 'Tosuke.'

"Anyway, I showed them these four items and they said, 'They are very unusual.' They also told me that it was impossible, from a historical point of view, for Shinran's writing to exist in Noto. They also said it would be problematic to find that Shinran's writing had been kept by an ordinary family and not by a temple, so it was not a simple matter. If it is Shinran's writing, then certain historical facts would have to be thrown out." His laugh entered his cup as he raised it to his lips, and I changed the position of my legs, which were beginning to feel like they had fused with the tatami.

He replaced his cup on the table. "Then I asked the two experts, 'So is it a copy or is it real?' And they asked me, 'What kind of family are you from?' I answered, 'We have a head family, but my own family is a branch and I'm the fifth generation.' 'Does your head family still exist?' 'Yes.' 'Where is your temple?' 'It's in Kabuto.' 'If this calligraphy is really by Shinran, how do you feel about it?' 'My own guess is that my grandfather, who was rather rich, bought it somewhere,' I said, 'because in my grandfather's time, twelve or thirteen people in Sora were involved in the shipping business. He was one of them, and there was a busy trading route between Nakai and Toyama. Sora was a port of call. I heard he earned a lot of money and often lent money to others.'

"Then one of them said, 'No, Mr. Morishita, your guess is wrong. Your grandfather was from the early Meiji era (1868–1912), and the man called Tosuke visited temples before your grandfather was born and, for some reason, far away from Noto. On reflection, it seems to me that these papers must have existed before your grandfather's time, so you have to treat them with care.' Then I realized he was right. It was at the beginning of the Meiji era that my grandfather had sailed across the bay to Toyama."

"Did they tell you whether it was written by Shinran or not?" Masako asked eagerly.

"No. He said he couldn't say anything. But when I asked 'Well, is this a copy?' he said 'It is by no means a copy.' But according to the researchers at the prefectural office, it is believed that nothing written by Shinran himself exists in Noto. On top of that, we are only farmers who own it, which complicates things.

"Eventually, they asked me to leave it with them, which I agreed to do. After that, my wife suffered from a very peculiar sickness. I don't understand the details, but something went wrong with her gullet. She had an operation at a hospital in Kanazawa. But even before the operation, the specialist said to me, 'It's no good.' He was very negative about her condition. When I asked what her chances were he said, 'One in four.' And he told me her sickness was very unusual, which meant they only knew of a few cases. Even if her life were saved, he said, she would lose her voice. This is what he told me about her case, and said, 'We will do our best, but you should prepare for the worst.' I was very depressed, but a young doctor who was directly taking care of my wife said 'Don't give up! Your wife will definitely recover.' Subsequently, the operation was a success and she didn't lose her voice, and after seven months in the hospital she came home.

"When we were first told of my wife's peculiar and serious sickness, my second daughter phoned me and said,

'Leaving Shinran's writing is like leaving *hotoke-sama* (Buddha) with other people and might have affected her. My husband's whole family thinks so, so why don't you ask them to return it to you?' I said, 'Stop bothering me!'" He laughed, shaking his head. "My eldest daughter and her husband, who are living with me now but at the time were living in Kanazawa, also agreed that Shinran's writing should be returned.

"Finally, I decided to talk about it with the head of the prefectural office. After listening to me, he said, 'We are keeping it as preciously as *hotoke-sama*. But if you are seriously thinking of keeping it yourself, we shall return it to you at once. But would you agree to our request to examine it again sometime?'

"So they returned everything to me. After the writing returned to the house, my wife's condition started to improve; of course this was after she had had the operation. Anyway, she was in hospital for seven months, and before she was discharged a strange thing happened. One day I was in the garden when I suddenly saw her standing in the gateway, wearing her ordinary clothes. But as I looked at her she just disappeared. I thought, that's very strange. Then I suddenly imagined that perhaps she had died and that a telephone call would come from the hospital, but nothing happened. Her apparition still puzzles me."

"Did she return home soon after you had seen her standing in the gateway?" I asked.

"Yes. Whenever I tell this story to other people, they think I imagined it and don't believe me. But she was definitely there in her everyday clothes; that's why I thought she had died.

"After that I began to think that that piece of paper had some kind of power and must therefore be genuine." He was slowly shaking his head to and fro, "I don't know . . . In Shikoku [famous for its Shingon temples] pilgrimages are famous, but I've never heard of the same thing in the Jōdo sect.

"Now, I'm wondering what I should do with Shinran's writing. This is my only worry. Financially I'm fine and I'm enjoying writing haiku."

While listening to his story, I had been convinced from the beginning that the most likely piece of Shinran's calligraphy, if indeed that is what it was, would have been the *nembutsu*—Amida Buddha's name written in six characters on a piece of paper, which may or may not have been mounted on a scroll. When I asked him if it was the *nembutsu*, he replied that it was and then suddenly launched into the story of how he originally discovered it.

"I remember that after my father died I moved the family Buddhist altar from his house to mine and something dropped out of it, which was almost completely black from age and the smoke from the fire. It was almost impossible to read what was written on it. I didn't even bother to put it back; I just rolled it up and left it like that in the altar.

"One day a friend wanted to see it, so we took it out into the light. He said, 'This is really something.' He was interested in antiques and knew more than me. He said, 'This is not an image of Buddha, it's a description of someone's calligraphy. Look, here it describes the sizes of the characters. You must have something extraordinary.' Then I said, 'It should be an image of Buddha.'

"After he read it through he said, 'This is a written statement about something.' This was the starting point of the matter of Shinran's calligraphy.

"Then I remembered an old box that my father had opened on special occasions. I showed it to my friend, and he carefully opened it. On the inside of the lid was a painting of a monk wearing a straw hat and carrying a staff. At the bottom of the box was a sheet of paper with some characters written on it."

His description of the painting resembled the general depiction of monks I had seen. "Is the monk Shinran?" I asked him.

"I think so, but there is no explanation about it. Anyway, my friend examined the papers in the box and said, 'The statement about the size of the characters is exactly right. I'm sure this is something extraordinary.' He said he would go and do some research on it at the Kanazawa library.

"After a while he phoned to say 'That calligraphy is indeed precious!' I said, 'Is it really? What shall I do then?' He replied, 'You don't need to do anything, just worship it. Don't make a fuss.'

"These days I'm wondering how my father had understood this, and what my grandfather had told him about it."

This all seemed to have been news to Max who, having been silent all afternoon, suddenly asked his uncle, "Do any other members of the family know about this? For example, does my mother know? It must be easier for you to talk about this kind of thing with women."

"I haven't told anyone. Mr. Murakami's old woman died the year before last at the age of ninety-five. Before she died I asked her if she had ever heard about it, but she said she had never heard anything about it. I also visited Mrs. Kawabuchi's old man and asked him if he had heard anything about it. His reply was, 'What a strange question. All the old people in the village know there is a treasure in your house. You shouldn't need to be asking about it, should you?'

"It was left in the altar, therefore I thought it was just an ordinary Buddha image. I never expected it to be something to do with Shinran's own calligraphy."

At that moment we heard the *genkan* door open and someone call. It was Max's wife, with the car to take Mr. Morishita back up the hill. We thanked him gratefully for his stories and asked if we could meet with him again, which he readily agreed to. It had begun snowing again as we walked across the little bridge to the car, and a wind was beginning to drive in from the sea.

For various reasons, we did not meet up with Mr. Morishita again. We phoned several times, but each time the phone was answered by another member of the family who said that he was out. Then our own busy schedules made it impossible to arrange to see him one more time before we left Japan. We hope to return to Sora in the near future, however, and see the calligraphy for ourselves.

> On a flag of water
> the voice of a ghost
> shakes the moon.

◆ Beached Bodhisattvas and Kami

A friend of ours, Naokazu Maruyama, has spent most of his life traveling around remote areas of Japan, photographing and writing about secluded Buddhist and Shintō images. Now in his seventies, he has written many books on the subject and over one thousand articles for one newspaper alone.

Once when he was staying with us during a visit to two temples in our area, he told me there were many, what he called "kami, from the outside" enshrined in Noto. The origins of these images is often far from the places they presently reside. While they consist of different types of images, they are known collectively as *hyōchakushin* (literally, "drifted gods or deities")—images of Buddhist deities or Shintō kami washed up on the shore or pulled from the sea.

He told me he had first learned of the images when he was traveling on the west coast of Hokkaido, looking for carved wooden images by the fourteenth-century itiner-ant monk-carver Enkū. He had discovered some images by Enkū in a Shintō shrine but was puzzled by the way that their faces had been completely worn away. The priest of the shrine told him that fishermen had thrown the images into the sea while they prayed for good herring catches. When the images drifted ashore or became caught in fishermen's nets, they were enshrined in their own villages as kami.

Some years previously, he said, he had found similar images of the Kamakura period (1185–1333), during which some of the finest Buddhist images were produced, enshrined in the Suzu shrine in the small port town of Suzu at the far-northern end of the Noto Peninsula. In the past Suzu had been an important port of trade and intercourse between the east and west sides of the Japan Sea coast.

Village archives record that since 1191 the Kaji family in Sora has been the guardian of such an image, a stone figure of the bodhisattva Jizō. According to the story, three men from the village were out fishing in the same boat one day and one of them tried to draw in the net, but it proved too heavy for him. He then asked one of the other men to help him, but their efforts still were of no avail. They thought it must have gotten caught on some rocks, so they asked the third man, who was an ancestor of the Kaji family, to make an attempt at raising the net. As soon as he put his hand to it, it began to come up very easily. When it was halfway into the boat, the two men who had originally failed to lift it wanted to take over, but again it proved impossible for them to move it. It was left to the Kaji's ancestor to pull in the remainder of the net, at the bottom of which, they discovered a stone image of Jizō. The other two men understood that the reason for the Kaji ancestor being able to raise the net was that the Jizō wanted him to look after it. Since then the Kaji family have remained the custodians of the image, which to this day is enshrined behind their house in a Jizō shrine that was last rebuilt in 1874.

No one among the present generations in the village has actually seen the image, as it remains hidden within its shrine; however, Rev. Tani's father, who was once Sora's village priest and is now a priest in a village temple some miles away, claims that the carved image reveals exposed breasts (a very unusual feature for such an image). He thinks this suggests it may have been placed in the sea by the grieving parents of a baby who had drowned.

There is a story concerning the Jizō that is part of Sora's own folklore, though how old this story is, or what its origins are, no one seems to know. It tells about a big fire that once engulfed the village, and while it raged through the houses in the main street, a huge man looking like a boatman appeared from nowhere and stopped the fire in front of the Kaji's house. The villagers understood him to be a manifestation of the Jizō, and since then, every year on the anniversary of this incident, the village has held a festival for the Jizō.

One year, however, a very long time ago, the weather was so bad they had to cancel the festival. The next day a man who had sailed over from Noto Island said to one of the villagers, "You must have had a wonderful festival last night."

"What makes you say that?" asked the villager.

"Because we could see a red glow all over Sora and reflected in the sea."

The villagers were very shocked and took it as a warning from the Jizō for having canceled the festival and, presumably, as a reminder of the fire. They determined never to break the continuity of the festival again.

Originally, the festival was held every year on August 23, but in recent times the date was changed to the fifteenth, because at that time family and relatives return to the villages from the cities to celebrate *obon* (a three- or four-day festival when the souls of the ancestors are said to visit the village and take up residence in the family Buddhist altars).

Late on the afternoon of the festival, the Jizō shrine is opened so that villagers may come and "greet" the Jizō, light incense, and leave a small donation if they wish. Then in the evening, Rev. Tani, or whoever the incumbent priest is, comes to the shrine and chants before its altar. With him, carried on a bier by four men, is a small *sakaki* tree (sacred to Shintō) mounted on a large, hexagonal mandala-like tray. Strips of white paper folded in a zigzag are attached near the top of the tree, symbolizing the presence of the kami, which here is actually the Buddhist bodhisattva Jizō, who is understood to have been transferred from the shrine to this sacred construction. The object in which a kami is said to reside—in this case the tree mounted on the mandala-like tray—is referred to as the *go-shintai*, or "the body of the kami," where it will remain for the duration of the tour of the village. The tree itself, I suspect, although no one in the village could tell us, represents the World Tree or Axis Mundi (that connects heaven and earth), linking it with early shamanistic practices. Here is a classic example of the fusion of Buddhist and Shintō elements and beliefs.

In the past, the *go-shintai* would have been accompanied by a number of special tall lanterns, often painted with images or calligraphy, but on the two occasions we witnessed the festival, candles were mounted on the *go-shintai* itself to light the way for the kami. The candles had been lit from the ones on the altar in the Jizō shrine. After the chanting, the *go-shintai* then visits the *genkan* of each house in the village while the priest chants at the family's Buddhist altar within. Afterward, the family makes an offering of rice which is poured into a big sack carried on a barrow behind the *go-shintai*.

Each year a family is asked if they will act as hosts to the *go-shintai*, the priest, and his entourage as they rest on their rounds. In our second year in the village, we were asked by Rev. Tani to perform this office, and we gladly agreed. We prepared snacks and plenty of beer and saké and set up a small altar on a table in a room between the *genkan* and the room containing the house altar. On the altar we placed our offering of rice on a traditional altar receptacle and set a small ceramic bottle of saké in the rice, with its neck stoppered with a *sakaki* leaf.

When the men arrived, they remained outside with the *go-shintai* while Rev. Tani came in and chanted in front of our altar. After chanting, he turned with a relaxed smile on his face, peeled off his robes down to his underwear, which were soaked through with sweat, and sat on the tatami to enjoy a smoke and a glass of chilled beer while I hung his robes in front of an electric fan to dry.

Once he had rested, he replaced his robes and the people waiting outside were invited into the house with the *go-shintai*. After a short service in front of the *go-shintai*, everyone relaxed and chatted while they drank, ate, and smoked. Various neighbors came and went until it was time for the *go-shintai* to move on and complete its rounds of the village.

Mr. Sakashita from across the road, who, unknown to me at the time, was soon to become the new headman, returned to our house with a bottle of saké. We sat up till late drinking and talking, long after the sounds of chanting had left the night air and until we were quite drunk.

> I *have listened to the stories*
> *told by fox and*
> *stream and star.*
> *And they all say—*
> *You are*
> *who you are,*
> *but not who you think*
> *you are.*

◆ The Saucepan Incident

I was working upstairs one morning, when I heard someone talking excitedly and loudly down below. Because the
voice was pitched high with emotional tension, I could
not tell at first whether it was a man or a woman. Listening carefully, I decided that it was a man and that Masako
was questioning him with a tone of concern in her voice.
A few moments later, I heard Masako phoning from the
middle room below, and a voice I now recognized as Old
Man Gonsaku's coming from the same room, though his
thick Sora dialect made it difficult to catch any words
from where I was.

I was just getting up from my desk on the hint that
something was wrong when Masako called up the stairs
to say Mrs. Fukada had been injured. By the time I arrived
downstairs, Old Man Gonsaku had returned to his own
house and Masako was making for the *genkan*. "Mrs.
Fukada's injured her head. She needs to go to the clinic."

We took the car across the road and parked it outside
their house. Standing outside their open door, we could
hear a row going on inside and Mrs. Fukada shouting, "I
don't need to go. The blood's stopped already."

Then Old Man Gonsaku replied, "Even if the blood's
stopped, you have to go to be checked. Because I hit you,
I'm coming with you."

"No! You don't need to come."

"I hurt you. I have to come. I have to tell the doctor
what I've done."

Eventually the shadows of their two bodies appeared
at the interior, dark end of the corridor as they moved forward toward the light of the *genkan*. Then gingerly holding
onto the door jamb, Mrs. Fukada stepped out onto the
road. Her hair was sticking up and sticky with a mess of
half-dried blood, and her face was red with the overflow
of her internal tide. It had splashed and run over her
sleeveless jacket and down her trousers. She looked like
an old chief at the Battle of Wounded Knee.

We got Old Man Gonsaku into the back of the car and Mrs. Fukada in the front, where she sat with a strange fixed smile on her bloodied face. All along the road, they took turns in repeating the lines of the drama.

"I wounded my wife."

"He didn't need to hit me so hard!"

When we arrived at the clinic, Old Man Gonsaku took his wife straight through to the treatment room. The nurse told him they did not need him and that he should go and sit in the waiting room. He wandered into the waiting room, turned around, and wandered straight back out and into the treatment room, where he was ordered out again.

He returned and sat down on a raised part of the floor that had been laid with tatami. We were the only ones present, since it was already lunch time, and he addressed us from where he sat, "My *babā* is hurt because I hit her. Blood came out of her head," he said, his hands indicating a fountain from the top of his head.

While he was out of the room, Masako had turned off the television set. He surveyed the dead screen, "Was the television off before?"

"No, I turned it off," said Masako.

He looked up at a large electric clock on the wall. It was 12:16. "I usually watch a quiz program about legal matters. I learn a lot from that program." He switched the television back on and sat directly in front of it, cross-legged on the tatami with his nose almost touching the screen. He had mud and dried grass stuck to the soles of his bare feet and a small package had mysteriously emerged from the bottom of his left trouser leg. When he noticed it, he giggled for the first time that morning and explained that he had a hole in his pocket. He thrust his arm down through the pocket, the length of his trouser leg, until his fingers appeared as strange neighbors to his toes, and retrieved the small package back up the trouser leg into the hammock of his torn pocket. A few minutes later while his mind was lost deep in legal questions, the package reappeared and its contents of black beans spilled over the tatami.

On having it pointed out to him, he carefully scooped them up in his hands and returned them to their wrapper. Then, standing up, he said, "What's going on in there?" And disappeared back into the treatment room.

A nurse's voice filled the building, "Old man, there's nothing for you to do here."

He returned once more and described the drama all over again, tears running down his face and mucus from his nose, which he wiped on the palm of his hand and then transferred to his trousers.

"Were you cooking or was Mrs. Fukada?" Masako asked.

"Me. I tried to cook daikon radish leaves with a mackerel head. We ate the body yesterday. I was going to use a saucepan I bought the other day. It was burned inside, and had been scraped with something sharp, not a pan cleaner, so I called to my *babā* and said, 'Why did you do this? You must have used a knife to scrape it.' She said no, but it was obvious that she had used a knife. She had already made a hole in the other one, which was why I bought the new one. I got very angry and hit her over the head with the saucepan. And then a lot of blood came out of her head, which she tried to catch in her hands but it overflowed onto the tatami. It's covered in blood. Then I tried to find someone to help and I saw your car was there and came to you."

Unable to remain in the waiting room with his guilt and his fear and remorse, he went back into the treatment room. After only one or two minutes he reappeared again with the latest bulletin, "Now they're going to x-ray her head."

He went back again. When he returned, after a slightly longer period this time, he said that after completing the x-ray and having the nurse clean her face and hair, he had offered to cut Mrs. Fukada's hair when they got back home. But he had been told that on no condition was he to do so. The hair was very important. He mustn't touch her head or her hair.

Sometime after the end of the legal quiz, and during a commercial for something that nobody in their right mind would want, the doctor appeared with a stitched up Mrs. Fukada. "Old Man," the young doctor said, looking sternly at Old Man Gonsaku, "you must have been drunk this morning."

"Yes, one cup of saké. Then fifteen or twenty minutes later I wounded her."

"That's right. Saké's no good."

"That's right," echoed Old Man Gonsaku, looking up at him like a guilty child. "Saké's no good." He remained staring up at the doctor as though waiting, wishing for some form of rebuke. The doctor was prosecutor, judge, and priest for him. He wanted to be accused, punished, and forgiven in the same breath.

A nurse came out with a big bag of medicine and tried to give it to Mrs. Fukada, but Old Man Gonsaku intercepted it, saying, "I'll look after it." The nurse carefully explained how and when it should be administered.

Returning to the village, it had been quiet in the car. The strong smell of medication seemed to have sedated their tongues, or at least created an intermission for the time being, with its alien smell of external intervention in their personal domestic drama.

The following morning, which was Sunday, Mrs. Fukada had to go to the clinic for a check-up. In the car she grumbled, "I can't stand to live with that old man anymore. I want to go to an old people's home. Whenever he's drunk he gets angry very easily. Even when he was young, any small thing could send him off."

"It's not always comfortable at an old people's home, though," Masako said to her. "At least at home you can do what you want."

"Yes," replied Mrs. Fukada thoughtfully, "that's right."

There was silence. Then, "He always complains about my cooking. He should stop complaining and just eat. Even a tiny bit. His own cooking isn't very good."

Suddenly, as we approached the school, there, coming up fast through the windscreen toward us, was Old Man Gonsaku pushing his bicycle. We stopped and wound down the window. "Where are you going?" Masako inquired.

"I'm going to Kabuto. But not to see my old *babā*." He spoke to Masako and I as though no one else occupied the car. And Mrs. Fukada ignored him as though he might have been a stranger we had asked for directions.

"Take care, then."

As we drove on, Mrs. Fukada murmured, "What's he going to Kabuto for? What reason?"

The possible reason presented itself to us later that day, when he arrived in our *genkan* with a polythene bag in one hand and a large bottle of Sōgen Saké in the other. The bag looked as though it contained a nimbus cloud but in fact two squid, with one eye staring out accusingly through an ink spattered side.

He sat down in the *genkan*. "The bottle is for husband and the squid are for wife, so you can eat them yourself on your own," he said, looking up at Masako. Then he repeated, "The saké is for husband." And a tear trailed down his right cheek.

The next day Old Man Gonsaku appeared again at our door, this time with a gift of jackfish (*aji*) and a tone of appeal and contrition in his voice. After the anxiety and guilt over the last forty-eight hours had begun to lose their emotional grip, concern about his image in our eyes had begun to establish itself. "I didn't hit her on the head with the saucepan," he said, tensing the muscles between his eyebrows so that a knot appeared above his nose, as though truth and sincerity were concentrated there. "I just covered her head with it. The pan has a dent in the bottom. That must have been what did it. I'm very happy my old *babā* doesn't feel any pain."

Tears once more contact-lensing his eyes, he returned back over the small bridge, convinced in his own mind that he had reorganized reality and restored himself.

◆ A Visit to Myōsenji

We were on our way to the village of Myōsenji, which bears the same name as the temple below which it was originally built, to visit a retired school teacher called Mr. Ichigan. We had been told that Mr. Ichigan was the person who could tell us about Stone Buddha Mountain, a confusion that had arisen between ourselves and Mr. Nagao when we asked if he knew the school teacher mentioned by the farmer we had met after looking at the stones on Stone Buddha Mountain. In Mr. Nagao's mind the image of "stone Buddha" had connected with a temple called Myōsenji, which has many stone images in its compound and on the hill behind it.

I already had intimations that a misunderstanding had arisen by the fact that Myōsenji is a long way from Stone Buddha Mountain and that the school teacher mentioned by the farmer was supposed to live in the village nearby.

I noticed as we turned off the main road and entered the village that there were some very old Jizō figures and an image of Kannon by the roadside. As we proceeded along the village street, we tried to guess which house might belong to Mr. Ichigan. As we drew level with our guess, I slowed down and asked a woman who was walking toward us to confirm our choice.

"Yes," she said, "you can park your car over there,"

pointing to a space where the road widened on the left side. She walked into the yard of the house, in front of us, and told us that she was in fact Mrs. Ichigan. She was dressed in traditional farmer's clothes and had a bright, clear ruddy face—like a calendar of early mornings and the weathers of all seasons. Her body was spare from the constant physical work of farming. Looking up at her as I removed my shoes in the *genkan*, I could almost feel the rhythms in her body of planting, cutting, patting rice balls, kneading wheat flour, chopping vegetables, and lifting and slapping wet mud up onto the banks of rice fields in early spring—all the rhythms by which domestic and agricultural tasks are performed, as varied and integrated as the flow of the seasons that demand these activities and dictate the ingredients of meals.

She showed us into a room to the left of the *genkan* where two men were sitting at a table. We greeted each other in the formal Japanese way: kneeling with our hands on the floor in front of us. Masako's hands were flat-palmed to the floor, a triangle to her forehead as she bowed; mine were fisted, with knuckles to the tatami, head bowed and almost touching the floor.

Mr. Ichigan, after introducing himself, introduced his companion as Mr. Kosugi, a childhood friend. Both men wore spectacles and, while obviously about the same age, Mr. Ichigan's hair had turned gray, while Mr. Kosugi's, unless he dyed it, was still crow-black. In the course of our meeting, they echoed and shared many habits of movement and attitude, with the kind of symbiotic ease of two people who have grown up in the same environmental womb together, side-by-side from their earliest days.

After quickly establishing that Mr. Ichigan knew nothing about Stone Buddha Mountain, there was an awkward hiatus. Neither of the men spoke, except, as usual, that Mr. Ichigan told me to relax and that I did not need to sit formally. A foreigner, particularly a man, is not expected to be able to sit in the formal Japanese position for any length of time; however, I had always found it a particularly comfortable way to sit—at least for up to an hour—and told him so.

In the rather awkward silence that ensued I discreetly looked about the room. Outside the window hanging from the lintel were two small bamboo cages, each containing a finch of some kind. They kept up a frenetic hopping from one perch to another, accompanying the movement with a "peep-peep-peep," which had an almost electric buzz-tone to it, each time their feet contacted a perch. On the opposite wall to where I was sitting and behind Mr. Kosugi there was a shelf stacked with papers and a small chest of three or four drawers. Mr. Ichigan sat with his back to the window, with a tray of cups, a vacuum flask, and a teapot beside him.

The atmosphere of rather stiff and polite conversation that had developed was broken every so often by Mrs. Ichigan bringing in plates of sweets and some biscuits and cakes we had brought as a gift.

I asked Mr. Ichigan if he minded me using a tape recorder. He said he had no objection, but when I tried to switch it on I found that the batteries had gone flat. I brought out my notebook instead and asked Masako to record any conversations that I would lose track of.

Since Stone Buddha Mountain was not something for discussion, I decided to ask him about their local village festivals. The Noto area is unique in using very tall four-sided lanterns (*kiriko*), sometimes mounted on wheels and pulled through the streets or on biers carried on the shoulders of young men. The biers are decorated with calligraphy or, on some occasions, with figures of various kinds. The main purpose of the *kiriko* is to light the way for the *mikoshi*, which becomes the temporary abode of the kami for the duration of the parade around the parish.

Mr. Ichigan removed his glasses and wiped something

away from one of the lenses. Then, replacing them, he said, "We hold festivals in the spring and autumn. At the spring festival we pray for a good harvest, and at the autumn festival we hold a thanksgiving. Both festivals relate to farming but, for some reason, after the war fishermen began to join us to celebrate together. Since then, after we've carried the *kiriko* around the village, we dip them into the sea.

"We have five *kiriko*. Each is about ten meters high. We decorate them with the family crest on one side and calligraphy on the other. We used to compete with each other with our decorations, but these days we only use three *kiriko*, due to the lack of people to carry them. Even with these three, we have to ask for help from the people in a nearby village.

"About sixty years ago, my father learned the Tengu Dance on Noto Island, and it was decided to include it in the festival, following the Lion Dance (*shishimai*). It's a dance where boys wear girls' kimonos. In fact, the festival used to be only for men, not women, and the women weren't allowed near the *mikoshi* or the *kiriko*." He smiled. "But, you know . . . lack of hands again, these days girls participate.

"You'll notice some big stones at the side of the road in the village. They are resting places for the kami (I suspect, more likely rest for the bearers!), when the *mikoshi* tours the village on festival days. Where the road is too narrow for a stone we make triangular piles of sand from the beach, which purifies that place.

"A long time ago the *mikoshi* was not only carried around the village but also around the rice field in front of Myōsenji temple. That field has a spring in it, and the name of the field is *butaida* [stage rice field—this must allude to its past use as a site for staging Noh plays, usually performed for the kami, which probably indicates the temple once shared its compound with a Shintō shrine]."

While he had been speaking, a wonderful smell of toasting *mochi* (cakes made from rice that has been pounded to a glutinous consistency) had filled the room from the kitchen, and Mrs. Ichigan came in with a plate piled high with them.

When each had been supplied with a *mochi* cake, we began to discuss the problems faced by agriculture, both in Japan and Europe, with the changes in cultural orientation and the way agriculture is fast becoming and, in many places, has already become purely a consumer industry and no longer a way of life. This led Mr. Ichigan to reminisce about his youth.

"Each family owned a bullock. Looking after the bullock was my job when I was young. In those days, at dawn on August 14 [*obon*, when the spirits of the dead return to their former homes], we used to take our bullocks down to the shore and bathe them in the sea. We enjoyed it very much.

"I think we used to bathe them to show our appreciation for their labor and to purify them. In the springtime they used to get covered all over with mud from working in the rice fields. And after work they had to sleep in such a small, dark place. We boys and the bullocks used to enjoy our time together. It was a short break for us all, before the autumn harvest."

As he talked, he would turn now and again to Mr. Kosugi, who would smile and nod, as if the tidewater of memory swirled crystal clear across the table between them and then receded again, dark with mud, back over the edge of time—images from the past washing up in a gentle ebbing and flowing.

Mr. Kosugi fished up one of the images and reminded Mr. Ichigan, "When we were small we used to make all our own toys. Our favorite was the *takeuma* ["bamboo horse," or stilts]. They were so high we could look in the windows on the second floor. And in the winter we used to race each other across the muddy rice fields." Each engaged the other's eyes in laughter.

I picked up another *mochi* cake from the plate. Crispy on the outside, with a faint burnt tang, which also fills the nostrils as you raise it to your mouth, and chewy on the inside—for a Japanese, a cake from childhood if ever there was one, and I suspect as powerful a mnemonic as Proust's famous madeleine.

Both men were beginning to relax, and I asked about the existence of any local natural healers in the area. This is a question that has always interested me. Even in areas as remote as these, Western scientific medicine has resulted in the almost complete disappearance of natural healers from the villages; however, as in the West, so-called alternative medicines are enjoying a popular revival, due to some of the negative side-effects of modern drugs. (In some areas in Japan there are hospitals and clinics that combine both Western medicine and traditional Chinese and Japanese therapies, which is the wisest approach.)

"I remember three men," Mr. Ichigan began, putting down his tea cup, which I noticed was decorated with a poem in cursive calligraphy. "There was one man," he said oddly, "who if he's still alive, must be 120 years old. He advised sick people to gather such and such a plant and boil it and drink the tea. Many villagers believed in him. Then there was a fortuneteller, but I don't remember him. But I do remember a bone-setter who now lives in Suzu and runs a clinic with his son. He used to be a policeman in Osaka and was a seventh dan in judo. He could give advice to people who were in trouble by reading their family graves." [A kind of oracle is obtained by reading the direction, shape, and general condition of a grave, the influence of which is said to impinge upon the welfare of the living members of the family concerned.]

Here, Mr. Kosugi said something to him about a particular grave in the village. "Oh yes. We have a grave in the village that's said to be the grave of Minamoto no Yoritomo [a major twelfth-century warlord]. Though why it should be here, I don't know."

"Didn't he establish the Kamakura shogunate in 1185?" Masako asked, changing the position of her legs.

"Yes, that's right. And he sent one of his vassals to control this area. Anyway, when Mr. Kosugi and I were small, we used to play soldiers around the grave, and one day we found a sword hidden in a length of clay pipe lying beside the grave. We played with it, but neither of us can remember what happened to it. Whether it was an ancient sword or not I don't know.

"Some years ago, a scholar came with a team from Kanazawa to excavate the grave. We found a Suzu-ware vase [pottery made in the Suzu area] that was in perfect condition." I noticed, from the periphery of my right eye, that Mr. Kosugi was making movements with his hands. I looked at him. He was making a form in the air of a woman's body, or maybe a cello, in describing the shape of the vase. Mr. Ichigan continued, "I think they expected to find bones in it, but as far as I remember there was only mud."

These excavated memories seemed to have energized them both. Initially reserved and shy, their faces were now shining and their bodies animated. Mrs. Ichigan, who now joined us, added her energy to the four of us by smiling, laughing, and nodding.

"Ichigan is an interesting name. It sounds like a monk's name."

"Yes. It's an unusual name. We're a branch of the Daibō family. Even so, my family goes back ten generations. Our ancestral house was built a bit farther down from this house we now live in. You probably noticed a Jizō image on your way here. Well, that image is called Ichigan Jizō. Just where you turn left into the village was where we used to burn the dead. Our ancestral home used to be close by. Our family name could have come from that Jizō but I don't know which came first.

"In the village we have three Jizō images. One is Ichigan Jizō, where you entered the village, and one is in the middle of the village, while the third is at the other entrance. It is the thirty-third Jizō of Myōsenji temple."

There was a slight pause while we sipped tea, ate more *mochi*, refilled cups, and I tried to free up the ink in my ballpoint.

"You must have seen many changes in the village," I said, once I had successfully trailed a black line across the top of a new page. It was then that I noticed the finches peep-peeping. Either they had restarted, or their calling had faded beyond my sensory range, like a ticking clock, and only now in this pause reached back into my awareness.

Mr. Ichigan was nodding. "The biggest change in village life is the decline in population, which can't be helped, because we can't live by farming alone anymore. Also, most of the old houses have been rebuilt.

"When we build a house, the most important thing is to keep a big space for gatherings, such as weddings and funerals.

"Talking about weddings, the most important part of a wedding is that before anything else the bride greets the bridegroom's family altar and shrine. When she comes to the bridegroom's house on the wedding day, the bridegroom's neighbors tie a rope across the road in order to obstruct her path to the house. Then her father has to give saké or a small amount of money to those people and ask them to let her in. This is our tradition. Greeting the ancestors of her husband-to-be and the kami is more important than the actual wedding ceremony itself."

Mrs. Ichigan had disappeared back into the kitchen briefly, and again there came the smell of toasting. In the meantime, there was a lull in the conversation and we started to admire the ceiling, which was decorated at its center with dark brown, shiny, and obviously very old stems of thin bamboo. Mr. Ichigan also looked up at the ceiling and pointed with his right hand. "This was my idea. When one of my relations demolished his old thatched house to build a new one, I asked him to give me the smoked bamboo that had lined the roof. They were smoked by many, many years of fires in the hearth. That's why they're dark brown. They're a good combination with the new bamboo, aren't they?

"After the Great Kobe Earthquake in January, experts pointed out the weak points of a Japanese house, such as no internal walls on the ground floor and a very heavy roof. It's true. As you can see here, all the rooms are divided by *karakami*, which are easily removed to make the rooms bigger. Anyway, according to those experts, having no inner walls and heavily tiled roofs was the major cause for the collapse of houses in the Kobe area.

"I agree with them, but in the case of my own house the carpenter built diagonal wooden boards inside the outside walls on the ground floor. And you notice how wide the lintels are. That's not for decorative purposes but essential to give strength to the structure, to protect our house in an earthquake."

As he stopped speaking, the finches' call returned. Looking at me, he suddenly said, "You can sit *seiza* [formally with legs folded under the body] for so long! I can't sit like that at all these days." He rolled up his right trouser leg. His own leg was pale and veiny, like a rolled map, and stuck all over with pieces of what looked like transparent tape, which reminded me of old stamp hinges. "There's too much pain in my legs. I have to have injections once a week."

Then as suddenly as he had drawn up his trouser leg, he said, "Come on, we'll show you Myōsenji temple."

In the *genkan*, we thanked Mrs. Ichigan for her kindness and climbed into the car. We followed Mr. Ichigan's small, white pickup the short distance to the temple.

Walking up the temple steps, he pointed out a huge, beautiful ancient wooden image of Amida Buddha enshrined within a large open-fronted building. We proceeded toward the Buddha hall and then to our left and beyond it where many small stone images were lying about the ground in various states of repair. We stopped in front of a large stone image of Jizō, about 130 centimeters in height. It was robed in a *kesa* of dirty white cloth, like an old tablecloth. Its face was missing, either through erosion or accident, and there was a stone basin full of rainwater at its feet.

"This Jizō is believed to heal eye problems. It is thought that if you bathe your eyes with water from the basin in front of it, whatever problems your eyes have will be healed. I don't know how many people believe it today, though."

We walked on up an embankment to where there was a small clearing to the left side of the path. There was a large, almost spherical rock with three small stones about the size of a man's fist nested on top of it.

"This stone," said Mr. Ichigan, "is believed to be a meteorite. It's about fifty centimeters in diameter, and the small stones on top of it, so it's said, will get rid of your warts if you rub them with one. I remember I came here often to rub my warts with them when I was a child, but I can't remember if it worked or not."

We came to a small hill with steps cut into the side and reinforced with small logs of wood. As we were walking up them, I noticed that Mr. Kosugi was lagging behind a bit and breathing heavily. I dropped back and asked him if he was all right. He smiled. "I'm all right . . . Smoking!"

When we reached the others, they were standing in front of a stone image of Kannon beside the path. "There are thirty-two images of Kannon on this hill. The thirty-third is in the village.

"It used to be said there were thousands of these images on this hill, but when we were small people began to pick up pieces of broken ones. They couldn't afford to buy proper gravestones in those days, so they used these. There are still a lot of remains in the grass, as you can see."

Coming down the other side of the hill past the line of Kannon images, I paused to look at the huge sweep of the temple roof and thought about all the thousands of monks who had trained and practiced there in the heyday of Japanese Buddhism.

It was getting late, the air was cold, and a very fine rain like cloud-dust was beginning to fall as we returned down the steps to the car. We thanked the two men for their hospitality and their stories, and as I wound down the car window, Mr. Ichigan said, "Mr. Ritchie, you are so big, but your car is so small!" We parted on laughter.

Just how closely the relationship between the temple and the village had been in the past is reflected in the names of the families of the village of Myōsenji, as written down for us by Mr. Ichigan. Here they are:

Akaike	red pond
Bettō	administrator of a large temple
Daibō	house of a great monk
Daibutsu	great Buddha
Daimon	great outer gate of the temple
Hasuike	lotus pond
Ichigan	one vow
Jizōdō	Jizō hall
Nyūdō	"entering the Way" (i.e., the Buddhist path)
Senbutsu	one thousand Buddhas
Terada	temple rice field
Torii	gateway to a shrine

◆ Beware of the Buddha

One day some friends of ours were about to go out shopping when they heard the bell on their Buddhist altar being hit twice. When they went into the room, they found their small son seated before the altar.

"What are you doing?" asked the mother.

"We're all going out now, so I'm asking the Buddha if a burglar comes in to bite him."

"How can the Buddha bite a burglar?" the puzzled mother asked.

Her small son pointed to the rice offerings on the altar. "Because if Buddha can eat rice, he must have teeth."

◆ Old Man Gonsaku's Inquiry

Snow hung on the breath of the air, and its rinds from the previous fall remained at the roadside the evening Old Man Gonsaku arrived at our house bearing a piece of paper with some Chinese characters written on it. He asked Masako if she could read it, since the meaning and reading of Chinese characters used in the Japanese language can be very difficult, even for the Japanese themselves. It was a very cold evening, and Masako invited him through to the kitchen where I was heating up a pan of saké on the stove.

It transpired that Old Man Gonsaku had spotted an attractive young woman working for the Pelican delivery company when she had stopped to deliver to the farmers' co-op, where he was enjoying his daily glasses of saké. There and then, he had decided that she would be a good match for his grandson, who also worked for a delivery company. We learned that the characters written on the piece of paper he carried was the family name of this young woman.

As he giggled over his hot saké, he asked Masako, "How do you read these characters? Iwabata? Or

Iwahata?" His throat was rough after breathing the cold air outside. After looking at Masako, he put down his cup and looked up at the ceiling.

Masako asked him if he knew which depot the young woman worked at, but he did not know, so she decided to phone the various Pelican depots. Using the phone book, she tried the one in Nakajima Town and asked if the young woman worked for them, but they did not recognize her name. She then phoned several other depots, none of which knew anyone by that name.

"Where did you get this name from?" Masako asked Old Man Gonsaku.

"The girl in the farmers' co-op, she wrote it down for me. You know, some days ago the Ueno's only son got married. But they're not living with his parents. They are living in the town. I think they will come back here when they get old. You are the same. You are not living with your parents.

"The farmers' co-op girl is now twenty-one years old, so I can ask her if she would like to meet my grandson. I'm like a detective or a policeman, aren't I?" he said, giggling and raising his head to look at us from beneath his hooded lids. "Today, I bought a big root of burdock in Kabuto to give some of it to you."

I offered him some more saké. "I've already drank saké at the shop in Kabuto, so just a little bit. My doctor always asks me how much I usually drink, so I decided to tell him one cup."

He suddenly noticed that his fly was open. Bobbing up and down with laughter, he said, "It's open here! I didn't feel chilly, but I've found it open. I went to Kabuto, came back, and then had a pee outside my house. Then I met your husband outside the fire-equipment hut, but I didn't ask him to read these characters for me. Although he might be able to read them," he giggled, and looked down at the piece of paper again.

"The girl in the farmers' co-op wrote it for me. I've asked her to meet my grandson so many times. She's never said no, but she's never asked me if she could meet him." Then as if to reassure himself and at the same time to make the situation sound more hopeful than it probably was, he repeated, "She didn't say no, you know. These days very few girls marry men from this area. The son in that big house is single, and the man next door to Katsuyama is also single, and Seibei's the same.

"When Ueno's son got married, they invited the mayor of Anamizu. The bride came from Fukushima. I heard that her parents are also farmers, though their house is near the *shinkansen* ["bullet train"] station. She said she could help the Uenos by working in their rice fields. Working in the rice fields these days, you know, they use machines. And they have a car . . ."

Masako, returning to the table from the sink, said, "We saw you the other day coming back from somewhere in very smart clothes."

"Me? In good clothes? Did you think I was a good looking man?" He giggled, "Then now you must be thinking I'm a strange looking man."

"No, you look very nice now."

"I'm always saying what comes out of my belly. I'm talking as it comes out of my belly."

"Isn't that how you've lived your life?"

"When I asked you the first time where you came from, you said Eikoku [Great Britain]. The character for Eikoku is the same as "rice" isn't it?"

Masako joined in, "No, that's America." She traced the character out on the table with her forefinger.

"Ah, I thought this," skating his finger across the table in front of him, "was Great Britain. During the war, the Shintō priest at Kabuto, I mean the father of the present priest, prayed for victory." He started to recite a Shintō prayer, giggling, ". . . *takamaga . . . tamae . . . kiyometamai. . . .*

It's such a long time since I've done it, I can't remember how to do it. When the priest was doing it he mentioned Eikoku and Beikoku [America]. I thought they were our friends, but . . ." He began to chant the prayer again and gradually "his belly" began to remember it as the giggles continued to bubble up from it.

"Sometime next May, I'll hold my father's memorial service. I've been allowed to live such a long time, but my father died when I was in my thirties. That's why his fiftieth memorial day is coming. And my mother's thirty-third memorial day is also next year. I'm thinking of holding both memorial services together.

"A long time ago, most people were dead before they could hold the thirty-third and fiftieth memorial services for their parents. I have to do it for both my parents like this while I'm still alive. I don't know how long I shall be able to live. . . . I have to hold the memorial service. . . . It's my duty.

"My brother is also still alive. He used to work for Mitsubishi. He's a great man. His wife was born just over there," he indicated a direction through the kitchen wall. "They decided to get married while they were at primary school together. Their parents were against them . . . but they decided. Both parents quarreled you know. They quarreled with bad words. But it was a long time ago."

He giggled, "I have to go home. B*abā* might be worried about me. When I was at the shop in Kabuto, she phoned there. I went there to buy burdock. You know, that kind of job takes time. I only had one cup of saké there and the phone went . . ."

He placed the piece of paper on the table and asked Masako to write the young woman's name in *kana* syllabary beside the Chinese characters, so he could remember how it was pronounced. "If *babā* asks where I've been, I'll show her this piece of paper and tell her I visited you here. She doesn't get angry. It was my fault I put the saucepan on her head . . . She seemed to be looking for me . . . Well, thank you. I'll bring you the burdock." And as good as his word, he returned half an hour later with the burdock and left it in the *genkan*.

> *Across the inlet,*
> *night falls*
> *off the edge*
> *of a heron's*
> *shout.*

◆ A Case of Karma

One evening, driving to my English class in Anamizu, I was just entering the town when I passed an empty car stuck fast into an electricity pole. Passing the same spot on my return home that night, the headlights of my car caught the colorful flare of a bouquet of flowers tied to the pole, where the car had been, signifying that the driver had obviously been killed.

A few days later, we learned that the driver had been a fishmonger from a village near Sora who frequently poached the territory around Sora village that belonged to our own fishmonger, a native of the village who lived just down the road from our house. His truck, which played popular songs (*enka*) over a speaker, transformed the village into a movie set for about half an hour each morning. Apparently, the two fishmongers had only recently exchanged words on the subject.

This information was relayed to us with the inference of a nudge that implied "You know, karma. . . ."

> *Without following*
> *—autumn*
> *comes after summer,*
> *and after winter—*
> *spring.*

◆ Mr. Muroki Brings a Photo

Spring arrived on the breath of the *uguisu* (Japanese bush warbler). The Japanese say that it's call—*hōhokekyo*—contains the title of the Lotus Sutra, *Hokekyō*. Its voice is pure and clear like the dawn of words, the origin of prayer. The best way to hear it is unexpectedly, when you are alone. The first time I heard it was from the other side of a *shōji* window during early morning meditation in a Zen temple. It was as though, in that moment, it had pronounced my whole being. Now this morning, its voice rang from the forest and over the roofs as I stood outside the house waiting for Mr. Muroki to arrive.

The morning air was soft and filled with small flyings and parachutings. In places, sunlight decanted down spider-lines, and the river released a strange bouquet that was at once as intimate as the scent of one's own skin and as mysterious and alien as the perfume of the sky might be.

Mr. Muroki was coming to deliver a photograph of himself. When I had tried to take a picture of him myself he had refused, saying that his hair needed to grow a little longer, for he had only recently had a very short haircut. His concern about his appearance surprised me at the time, and when I arrived with my camera some weeks later, he said that he preferred to give me a photograph that he already had of himself, when he could find it.

I heard his motorcycle coming through the village and a few moments later he appeared, passing over the bridge with his two sticks sticking out from the back of his bike.

Coming through the front door after our initial greeting, he said, "You were away for a long time."

As he maneuvered his sticks onto the *genkan* step and sat on it to change his shoes, I explained that we had been staying at a friend's temple in a village near Lake Biwa and then gone on to stay at the head temple of the Jōdo Shin sect in Kyoto. "Good," he said, following me into the kitchen where there were chairs. He had mentioned on the previous visit that it was more comfortable these days for him to sit on chairs rather than on tatami.

While coffee was being prepared, he took out his wallet and extracted something from it. "This is a negative of a photo of me. I do have a more recent one, but I don't like it. This one was taken about ten years ago for my driving license. Is it all right?"

I held it up to the light and we both peered at it. "It's very nice, Mr. Muroki. Thank you. We'll get a couple of prints developed in town and then return this negative to you."

"In this photo I was seventy-five. I was young," he laughed. Then noticing a collection of beach stones lying on the table, he picked one up and, looking at it, said, "This is a fossil, isn't it?"

"Yes, it's a piece of fossilized wood. We found it on a beach a few miles down the coast from Wajima."

As Masako brought the coffee to the table, I went upstairs and brought down a magnifying glass. He examined the stone through it, turning it over in his hand. "I have the same type of stone. My two sons found some in the sea in front of my house." He looked at it again with his head slightly to one side, centering his right eye above and within the frame of the lens. "Ah, I can see the age-rings. Lovely! I wonder how many millions of years old this is. You can see part of this stone is coal. Near my house there used to be coal. No, it wasn't quite coal yet. What do you call it? Lignite?" He furrowed his brow, "Yes, lignite."

He adjusted the position of his cup for milk to be added to his coffee. "I didn't know you were interested in Nishi Honganji [head temple of the Jōdo Shin sect]. With regard to the human mind, I think Buddhism is truly the religion for human beings."

I agreed with him. Then he added, "I don't think I understand the deep part of Buddhism. . . . I don't know why we dream. I dream every night. I often dream of people who've died. Recently I dreamed of my wife—three times, one after another.

"When I visited the hospital in Anamizu, I met a friend in the town and he mentioned a doctor near Kanazawa who might heal my leg. He said he would take me there the following day if I wanted to go, but I told him I couldn't make a decision without talking to my son.

"Speaking of dreams, the night before I went to Anamizu I dreamed of the small lamps in my Buddhist altar. I recently decided not to keep them switched on after my morning and evening chanting, and I remembered this in my dream. But when I saw the altar in my dream, the lamps were on. It was a strange dream.

"For years and years, I always kept the lamps alight all day long. But recently, I learned from the TV news that some houses had burned down because of electricity leaks in the altars; since then I stopped leaving them on.

"Anyway, before that dream, I dreamed of my wife three times. Reflecting on all these dreams, I began to imagine that my wife was telling me to visit the doctor my friend had mentioned. So sometime I want to go."

He was pointing at and prodding his leg with a finger. "These days the pain in my leg is moving from left to right. Initially, the problem was due to a slipped disc. Then it gradually affected my leg more. Recently, I began to wonder if it might be due to a stroke, because my mother died of one." I told him I doubted his problem was due to a stroke.

"My doctor once told me it was incurable," he went on. "I think a surgical operation is like a gamble. I don't know the exact position, but one of the discs has slipped somewhere in my lower back."

We talked about slipped discs and back pain for a while. Then he said, "Well, in fact, I've suffered from a slipped disc many times. There used to be a therapist in Anamizu who did electric acupuncture. Those days, whenever I had a problem I had his treatment and the pain would go away immediately.

"When I was still working at the council office in Anamizu I suffered badly and was hospitalized for two weeks, at the end of which the doctor said I had completely recovered so I left the hospital.

"Anyway, I got off the train at Kabuto Station and picked up my bicycle, which I had left there a long time before, and pushed it home. It was snowing that day and I felt so good that I almost rode my bicycle, but just to be safe I didn't. When I got back home the pain returned, and I had to go back to the hospital and stay there for a whole month. It was terrible! And when I came back again from the hospital it was a very busy time for farmers, and I worked very hard helping my wife in the rice fields and the vegetable garden each day, after my work at the office. Then I got the same problem, but I didn't go back to the hospital. I knew that one week to ten days of good rest would heal me.

"The last lower-back problem happened three or four years after my wife died, when I began to feel my lower back getting heavier and heavier. Eventually, the pain came to my left leg."

He sipped his coffee and picked up another stone. "How do you find such unusual things? Some years ago, one of my sons who now lives in Tokyo found the fossil of a shark's tooth in the sea. I can't remember where I put it, though."

Mr. Muroki fingered the stones again like a lapidary examining gems. Then he pulled a handkerchief out from a pocket. Wiping his nose, he spoke, barely before the handkerchief had left the wings of his nostrils, "The other day when I was in my futon with a cold, I tried to go to the lavatory with my two sticks, which I always keep beside my futon at night, but I found I couldn't even stand up. In the end, I gave up trying to use the sticks and crawled on

my hands and knees." He laughed shyly, "That was a terrible cold. I couldn't cook and I just stayed in my futon.
My neighbor brought me rice gruel. I ate it with *umeboshi*
[pickled plums]. After the *umeboshi* had gone down to my
stomach with the rice gruel, its flavor remained in my
mouth. I enjoyed it so much! I'm not sure whether it
healed me or not, but, I gradually got better anyway. I
realized again that *umeboshi* is wonderful medicine, just as
people in the old days used to say."

Some people were passing along the riverbank beside
the house. Their voices briefly entered the house on the
squeaking of a wheelbarrow, then receded again. A crow
murmured something from a nearby roof.

Mr. Muroki paused with his cup in front of his mouth,
the surface of the coffee reflecting his lips. "Since the
Great Kansai Earthquake, I have been wondering
whether we should change our understanding of the
story of Zenzuka. We're told that there was a great
famine during the Kyōhō period [1716–36]. In reporting
the recent big earthquake, the *Chūnichi* newspaper listed
great earthquakes of the past and where and when they
happened. According to this list, in the Kyōhō period
there was a big earthquake in Noto. And I began to wonder if it was this earthquake that caused the famine. I
don't know that as a fact, but at least we can guess that
it might have been so.

"Many other villages must have suffered from the
famine. But I imagine the people of Sora had to wait a
long time for relief—I mean, longer than other villages.
Sora didn't belong to the local lord of the Kaga domain,
but was fiefed directly to the Tokugawa shogunate. I don't
know why."

Suddenly the energy that had been concentrated
around this subject was short-circuited by his catching
sight of a small bamboo basket filled with stones that had
a natural hole through each of them. Stirring them

around in the basket with a forefinger, he exclaimed, "These are unusual!"

"We found some of them on a beach near Nishiho and some on local beaches near here," Masako explained. "When we were staying in Kyoto at Nishi Honganji's guest house, we visited another temple, where we saw a huge collection of stones with holes in them. The stones were offerings from people who were blind and deaf and wished to have their sight and hearing restored so that it would be so sharp it could even penetrate stone!"

Holding up one of the stones and looking through the hole, he said, "Well, I've never heard of that before."

The conversation traveled on to a discussion about the differences between the villages in the area. On the subject, Mr. Muroki said, "Don't you think Sora is different from other villages in this area? I myself was born in this village but left here with my parents when I was about ten. We went to Kobe to live and came back after the war. Then I got a job in the council office in Anamizu and consequently didn't have time to have contact with the village people until I retired.

"You know, after the fifty years or more since I came back here, the village people still think of me as a person who went away and then came back, even though lots of the local men spent most of their time working in the Kansai or Kanto areas and only returned twice a year to stay with their families for three or four days. Once you've sold your house and land, like my parents, it means you've abandoned your native land. Anyway, I think Sora is definitely different from Kanami or Kabuto.

"Our way of speaking is affected by the fact that lots of Sora people went away from home to earn money and were influenced by the people from those other areas. When they came back home, a small part of their way of speaking was a little bit different from the Sora way, then gradually family and friends picked it up from them.

"Some years ago, I recorded these kinds of word differences. My idea was to record our own dialect before it completely disappeared. I had this record published in the town magazine. Village people say that I still sometimes speak with a Kobe accent." He laughed. "In Kanami people tend to stay in their village. They are not like Sora people. There are lots of carpenters and builders in Kanami, and because those skills are combined with farming and fishing they don't have to go away to earn money. In the 1950s there were lots of opportunities to work in the cities, mainly on building sites and road constructions, which tempted a lot of poor farmers away from home.

"Up to that period we had relied on bullocks and our own hands to work the land. But then we started to buy machines, so we needed cash to buy them with. Kabuto people went to the Tokyo area and Sora people went to the Kobe area to work, so that is one of the reasons why the people of these villages speak slightly differently."

Masako offered him another cup of coffee, which he declined, explaining that if he drank too much it made him pee a lot. "The other day my feet became swollen and I went to the clinic in Kabuto. The doctor gave me some medicine that worked well for my feet, but since then I've tended to wake up in the night for a pee.

"Sometime ago, I went to bed without peeing first, although I needed to go. But it was too cold to go to the lavatory, you know. It wasn't good. Last night it wasn't too bad though. Sometimes I have to go to the lavatory three times. It's too much. The doctor told me to drink a large saké bottle of water a day. How can I? If I follow his suggestion, I'll have to spend all night going to the lavatory!"

We all laughed. Then I described to him how in Britain when I was a child everyone kept a pot under the bed or in a specially designed cupboard beside the bed especially for that purpose. In those days a high proportion of houses still had outside lavatories.

Through his laughter he expressed his surprise by raising his eyebrows. "Really? How convenient! In fact, the doctor suggested I keep some sort of pot beside my futon, but I said, no, it'd be too smelly!

"My eldest son is concerned about my toilet business. He is pushing me to convert my toilet [i.e., to a modern pedestal flush model]. Last year in fact he sent a builder to have a look. When he arrived to check it, he said that not only the lavatory but also the kitchen and the bathroom needed renovating. Then I thought to myself, I'm the only one who lives here. If I can be patient with the inconvenience of the toilet, there's no need to spend any money. I should make do.

"My daughter is also worrying, and she sent me a brochure of toilet conversions, which I thought quite nice. But my son didn't think they were any good. In the end, I gave up on the whole toilet business. I'm too old. There's no point in converting it just for myself. I told my son that even if the toilet was converted, the house itself wouldn't last very long. It would be ridiculous if the lavatory survived while the rest of the house fell down! I decided not to use the money for the toilet business but to save it, instead, to leave to the children. They will be delighted."

Returning his attention to the stones with the holes in them, the subject of superstitions came up. I found myself telling him about an old horse dealer I once knew in Cornwall who, if he saw one solitary magpie on his way to market or to do a deal, would turn straight around and return home, because a single magpie was said to portend sorrow. Mr. Muroki was unfamiliar with the magpie as a bird so I had to describe it to him, mentioning that it belonged to the crow family.

"In Japan we believe it's not good to hear a crow calling. [The crow being ubiquitous in Japan, as in most places, it is difficult not to!] It means a death will occur in the hearer's family. We still believe it these days.

"The day my brother died I remember a crow cawing terribly in the front of our house, just before we received a telegram telling us of the death. Later, we told each other that the crow was informing us of the bad news.

"In this village, people say that the family who suffers a loss doesn't hear the crow's calling but only the people around them, or their relatives."

"What about snakes?" I asked.

"Snakes are sometimes said to be kami. Before this house was built, there was a rice field on here. When my wife and I were preparing the ground for the house, a friend told us to be careful because a kami was living there. We had to dig out the old stubble and bring in new soil to make a good foundation. Since he told us, I thought we should take it very seriously so we were very careful. Anyway, a few days after our friend told us, we were moving a boulder when we found a snake underneath it, which quickly disappeared. We wondered if it was the kami.

"As you know, Helmet Mountain is beyond Kabuto primary school. It is said that a huge snake used to live there. I'll tell you some of the stories I heard from my friends when we old men gathered to chat.

"Genmatsu Ōshima, who lives in Kabuto, started by telling us that he saw a huge snake on Helmet Mountain. He said he thought it was a huge bough lying on the ground and stepped over it, but, he said, it suddenly moved. He ran back home and started drinking saké as though he wanted to drown himself.

"I also heard of someone's daughter-in-law and two other people who came across a giant snake on Helmet Mountain, and I began to believe in the snake myself.

"Then I told the old men about my own experience. When I was still working at the council office, a village person asked me if I still went through the tunnel on my way to Anamizu. I said, Yes, I use the tunnel every day.

Why?' And he said, 'Well, you'd better not.' It was a short-cut to Anamizu, and I knew that two people had been killed during construction of the tunnel.

"Sometimes in those days, fishermen's wives came from Wajima to Sora by boat to sell seaweed and fish. According to the man who had warned me about the tunnel, one of them was pulled into the tunnel by something and never came back. That's why he warned me. Somehow this story scared me, and since then I stopped using the tunnel.

"I remember a story about a monster. Do you know a village called Kawashiri?"

"Yes, it's near Bira," Masako replied.

"That's right."

"One of Malcolm's students lives there."

"Well, on the edge of the village there used to be the cremation ground. A man from the village told us that a monster used to live beside that place and that it loved sumo. It forced anyone passing by to do sumo with it, and one day it challenged a man who was walking by. But the man told the monster that they should do it in the village, otherwise no one would know who the winner was. When he suggested this, the monster suddenly disappeared and was never seen again."

There was a brief pause while he finished his coffee and munched on a biscuit. Then he said, "You know the holiday houses in Tsubaki-ga-Saki, don't you. Well, a little bit farther along from there is a spot called Futaomote. It's called that because we can see the sea on both sides. Anyway, on the cliff at Futaomote a man stepped over something that looked like a saké barrel, but it suddenly rolled down the hill, jumped into the sea, and swam across to Noto Island."

Suddenly he looked up, "What time is it?"

I looked at my watch, "Nearly twelve o'clock."

"Oh, is it? I really enjoyed talking. Thank you very much for letting me talk so much."

"Thank you for talking. We enjoyed your stories very much," I said as Masako gave him a bag containing some lunch she had prepared for him.

> *Showing no favor,*
> *sudden rain*
> *falls about the place—*
> *even drenching*
> *an old pond.*

◆ Talking Trees

I was cycling back from the temple when I passed Mr. Nagao carrying some one-meter lengths of *kunugi* oak into his shed across the road from his house. He told me he had just drilled them with holes and filled them with pellets containing the spores of the *shiitake* mushroom. He was going to take them the next morning up into his forest, where he would stack them so the spores would germinate. He invited us to visit him the following afternoon when, he said, an old friend of his who was a forestry expert would also be paying him a call. He suggested we all drink saké together.

As before, Mr. Nagao's room was very warm, but mercifully the television sat darkened and inert. We were introduced to Mr. Kakuma who offered me his business card. He was a small round man wearing a jacket and tie and seemed to have difficulty sitting on the floor for any length of time; he kept shifting his position and ended up propped against the wall behind him.

Mr. Nagao already had some saké heating on the stove and poured each of us a generous cupful. We raised our cups in "*kanpai*" and then Mr. Kakuma asked me if we had many forests in Britain. I explained that we had systematically destroyed all our ancient forests by using the trees initially for building houses and cathedral roofs but then, perhaps more devastatingly, for fleets of warships and their maintenance. Later we cut trees to make way for sheep in the Highlands, for the mills of the Industrial Revolution, pit props for mines, and charcoal for iron smelting. "For example, an Elizabethan house would take one to two hundred oak trees, and a cathedral, seven hundred to one thousand trees for a roof. A large wooden warship would take three thousand oak trees, which amounts to about seventy to eighty acres of timber. By the seventeenth century, our forests were already depleted."

I told him that we had now replanted commercial forests with cheap, fast-growing trees like Sitka firs, and that overall the policies with regard to forestry had been pretty disastrous for the environment generally.

"I would imagine the wood from those trees must be soft and coarse, isn't it?" asked Mr. Nagao, lighting a cigarette.

"Yes, you're quite right," I replied. "And very badly seasoned."

"In this area," said Mr. Kakuma, "we plant young trees close together and then leave them as they are for about ten years. Then we gradually thin them out so that the grain grows evenly. We have to leave them close together for ten years in order to stop them from growing too fast. The timber trade demands an even grain. Of course, a good natural environment and our careful work is essential in producing good timber for commercial purposes."

He moved into a cross-legged position with quiet grunts and a whistle in an unclean nostril. "Trees that grow in bad weather conditions are valued highly in the market. I'm talking about building timber. Japanese cypress [hinoki], for example, planted in bad places takes a long time to grow, usually three times as long as pine. Trees that have grown under difficult conditions are chosen for building shrines and temples. This is why they can survive for hundreds of years."

"What are the best 'worst' conditions for growing excellent cypress?" Masako asked, turning her cup around between her fingers.

Mr. Kakuma fidgeted, "First of all, it should survive years of severe winters—snow and wind . . ."

Only realizing after I had begun that I was interrupting him, I said, "Fascinating! I heard that in the old days when a master carpenter needed one of those massive ridge poles for a temple, he only had to look at the tree and he knew, without measurement, exactly where to cut it; and then when it was lowered into position, it would fit exactly. Is that true?"

"It's true, especially, of the master carpenters of shrines and temples. They could see intuitively which tree to use for which purpose before they cut it down. Those masters had an extraordinary ability to measure with their eyes only.

"For the main pillars of shrines or temples, trees from the worst areas are chosen. Timber that is used for the outside of the building, where it will be exposed to rain, snow, and wind, should also be grown in those kinds of conditions. Trees that grow on the sunny side of a mountain should be used for the interiors of houses. That means that the wood of the trees should remain in the same environment in which it grew. That's why Japan's wooden temples and shrines have survived for so long."

Mr. Nagao was visiting each cup with the spout of the saké kettle. While he carefully let the hot, clear liquid pour into the cups, he said, "Next time, I'll show you my mountain. I have cypress trees that are twenty-five years old."

"Mr. Nagao, thinking of the time it takes for a tree to grow, the trees you've planted will only be big enough to cut down in your grandson's time," said Masako, pushing an ashtray toward Mr. Kakuma, who had just lit a cigarette.

"Yes," replied Mr. Nagao, "Good wood needs sixty to seventy years to grow. About five years ago when this area was hit by a big typhoon, almost two thousand trees were blown down on my mountain. Many of them blocked the road, so I had to move them away and take them to the sawmill. The wood is still piled in my shed. I don't need to rebuild my house, so it's useless to me. I told many people to take it if they needed it. Mr. Ritchie, if you want to build a house you can have it all." We all laughed, and for the umpteenth time I fantasized about building a house on a remote site overlooking the sea.

"About ten years ago a man came from Kyoto and asked me to sell him one of my paulownias. I didn't want to sell it, so when he asked my price I jokingly said one million yen. He immediately agreed to buy. I was so shocked, I said, 'Give me time to think about it.' He replied, 'Are you a man? You must have balls. What a shame that after giving me a price you should ask me to wait while you make up your mind.'" He rolled back and forth with laughter, sending ash down his old padded jacket. "Eventually I sold it to him, and he told me that the wood near the root was used to carve a lion [*shishi*] mask, and that the upper part was used for making a *koto*.

"Later, a man from Wajima wanted to buy a zelkova [*keyaki*] tree from me and offered me ¥750,000. But I told him I wanted one million, and he said it was too much and gave up. After that, I decided to cut it down. While I was cutting it down it split right down the middle, and all I could get for it was ¥300,000 from a man in Anamizu. You see, that was punishment for being greedy!"

Mr. Kakuma was stubbing out his half-smoked cigarette. "It's a matter of how you went about cutting down a very hard tree like *keyaki*. You destroyed it by the way you cut it down."

"I remember my mother told me that in her native land, Niigata, when a girl was born the parents planted a paulownia so that it would be big enough to make a chest of drawers for her kimono when she got married," Masako said, holding her cup toward Mr. Nagao for a refill.

"Trees are like children," Mr. Nagao said, refilling the saké kettle after replenishing all our cups. "You have to look after them constantly."

Mr. Kakuma was spilling cigarettes all around the space in front of him as he shifted into a more comfortable position. As he gathered them up, he said, "Spirits dwell within trees. People like Mr. Nagao look after trees with all their hearts, not for themselves but for the trees, as well as for their families two or three generations ahead."

"In Britain we talk about genealogy in terms of a family tree, and we describe the different lines of a family as branches," I said.

Mr. Kakuma had fitted all the cigarettes back into the pack except one, which bobbed, unlit, up and down between his lips as he spoke. "Is that so? It's interesting that you use the tree to explain your blood relations. We use the Chinese character for house.'"

I excused myself for a trip to the toilet. As I opened the *karakami* into the hallway, the cold air felt like I had entered a mountain pool from a side door, after the airless heat of the room. The cold air made me realize how drunk I was beginning to feel.

As I reentered the Martian atmosphere of the room, Mr. Nagao was saying, "Until the late sixties I had a fishing boat, but I sold it in order to concentrate on forestry and on my rice fields. Some years ago, though, I bought my son-in-law a boat. He often takes his three sons fishing. The reason I stopped fishing was that it took too much from me physically. I began to realize that the salty wind took a lot of my energy."

There was a noise in the hallway, and his youngest grandson poked his head around the *karakami*, announced "*Tadaima*" (I'm back), and screwed up his face. "What's the matter?" I asked. "I hate the smell of saké," he replied and closed the *karakami* again.

The conversation turned to catching sea cucumber, a

local delicacy. The fisherman leans over the side of his boat and peers onto the seabed through a glass-bottomed box. When he spies a sea cucumber, he grips it with the aid of a bamboo pole, the end of which has been split into three prongs.

"Here we are very lucky to have so much food free from the sea, as well as from the mountains." Mr. Nagao was holding the saké kettle again, and we were dutifully emptying our cups with swift gulps.

"It's the best way to live," said Masako.

"But it's very difficult, too." Mr. Nagao was lighting another cigarette. "Because we have to earn money. We want to drink saké and we want to drink beer. If we could get them both from the tap, no problem. Or if we could swap rice for saké, it would be wonderful!" We all laughed, cigarettes and ashes flying, and saké beginning to work our limbs.

"What worries me is that village life like this is going to disappear very soon. Japan has really lost its culture. But what remains of it, I believe, is in villages like this." Mr. Nagao was grinning broadly and nodding his agreement at me.

"I agree with you!" said Mr. Kakuma emphatically, as he tipped himself back against the wall, bringing his legs from under him into a cross-legged position again.

"Once there were ninety-seven occupied houses here, which means there are now some twenty houses that are empty. Some families have completely died out because they were childless, and some have moved to the city. I think in ten years time the population of this village will have fallen to half. In the past, we could live very easily. I mean we could fish . . . . there were lots of fish in those days. If we had a tiny bit of money, we could eat with no problem. We had rice and vegetables and we produced our own saké. Of course, we made it secretly!" Mr. Nagao stopped and looked up as his wife put her head around the *karakami* and dropped a bag of sweet potatoes at Masako's feet. She smiled and disappeared again.

Mr. Nagao continued, "Eating, living, working, everything, even the house itself is beginning to change here. I don't know whether it's modernization or what it is. We need money for everything these days. The whole system demands money." Mr. Nagao's arm was poking at the air and cracking with each movement as though he was firing off his frustration.

"We have to make an effort to keep our traditions," asserted Mr. Kakuma, bending over another cigarette.

"It's strange to me that the objects we used to use for everyday living have now become ornaments," laughed Mr. Nagao. "For example, the other day I went to a place in Anamizu and there was a pot-hanger that we used to use over the hearth, hanging in the corner of the room as an ornament." His face was taut with a mixture of pain and incredulity.

Yes," I said. "It's a bit like looking at the bones of a dead culture, isn't it?" Mr. Nagao nodded morosely.

Then Mr. Kakuma asked, "What about Britain?"

"It's exactly the same there. Except we're a few a steps ahead of you in the business of cultural suicide. The true cultures of Europe probably began dying long before the so-called Age of Enlightenment in the eighteenth century." I could feel the surf of an alcoholic wave under my breath. "My definition of culture is perhaps a little idiosyncratic, I don't know. But in English, the Latin root of the word 'culture' means to till the earth, and it's my belief that once you lose that rootedness, that respect and dependence on Nature and contact with the land, or imagine you can dispense with it, then you've lost the true meaning of culture. It's from the rhythms, sights, sounds, smells, tastes, and touches of our environment— and most importantly where we feel at one with them— that all our senses of music, poetry, dance, our old sciences of wonder, and so on, and our sense of the divine has come. True cultures are holistic." I was at full gallop—my hobby-horse tearing along on rather numbed hooves. I wasn't quite sure where it might go next.

"I think it's the integration of all the activities of living—whether domestic, mundane, artistic, religious, sacred, or whatever—directed toward the Absolute, or whatever you want to call it, that creates true culture. What I mean is at some level of understanding there's no differentiation between all these different ways of manifesting ourselves. Everything that exists cannot ultimately be anything but Buddha, or the Absolute. I don't believe there can truly be such a thing as a secular culture in any real sense. Today we live impoverished lives, with all our so-called wealth, and have reduced our cultures to clusters of trading and competing consumer societies. Culture is dead. Don't forget, Japan is now described as 'Western' on the world scene. I know that 'East' and 'West' are just convenient labels, but it does indicate something of the condition of your own culture, don't you think? The direction we're headed in now doesn't bode well for any kind of future." I was trying to rein in. I knew I was drunk and was aware that anyone a little more sober might knock holes in some of my statements. But as I looked around the table, it was as though I was passing their faces at speed. We were all too drunk to analyze what I was saying, and all along for the ride because the rhythm felt right. It was when I heard Masako attempting to interpret that I realized that somewhere along the road I had verged into English.

"How did you learn the word *shōrai* [future]?" asked Mr. Nagao, nipping off the glowing bud of his cigarette into the ashtray between his forefinger and thumb.

"From listening to people talk. I'm sorry I keep using English, but I'm a bit stupid and I have big holes in my Japanese," I said.

"Don't worry. I really understand. It must be difficult."

My horse seemed determined to go farther down the road yet, so I continued, "The problem in Europe has been the destruction of farming as a way of life and its debasement to a consumer industry. We've killed the land with chemicals till it has developed a dependence on them in order to be able to function and produce the yields demanded by the markets. We've turned the land into a junkie.

"Another problem with the death of rural culture is the increasing suburbanization of the countryside—people moving from urban and suburban areas, carrying an idea or an image of living in the countryside when they don't realize that they don't actually like the reality of living there. The smells, the mud, the shit of cows and pigs, the noise of cockcrow in the morning—they even write letters to their local papers complaining about it. They want double glazing, macadamized lanes, electric lights in the garden, anything to lessen the threat of actually living alongside the unpredictable. There is even a magazine in Britain to show you how to live in the countryside. It's like a kind of fashion magazine. It shows you how to look, how your house and garden might look, how the houses of fashionable people who live in the countryside look, and so on. And it's mostly filled with advertisements for things to help you with your image of living in the country-side. We've turned country life into a commodity to sell. We're motivated by attaining the image of some-thing rather than the actuality because we've forgotten what it was . . ." I could tell by the weary expression on Masako's face as she looked at me that I was either bor-ing everyone with my usual line of prejudices or had strayed over the linguistic border again, or both of these. She began to summarize some of my main points. I tried to add the rider that not everyone who moved from the cities was like this of course—some truly lived in the countryside—but that in our image-oriented society this was the big problem. I could tell from the tone in her voice, however, as she continued to interpret my previous spiel over what I was now saying, that she was going no further with it.

"Why are we moving away from the land in Japan?" asked Mr. Kakuma through a cloud of cigarette smoke.

"Because you willingly caught a very pernicious disease from the West," I said holding up my cup as it was refilled. "The agrarian and industrial revolutions could only have had their origins based somewhere down the line on a dualistic, patriarchal religious doctrine. I believe they could only have begun in Europe, as they did, in fact, in my own country. I don't believe they could have started in, say, a Buddhist or Taoist culture. If we look behind us, we can see the stepping stones that led us to where we are in all this. But because you caught it from us, if you look behind you, it's rather confusing—like someone who's had acid dropped in their tea or taken a trip to the other side of the world in a jet. It's suddenly all this, and how did we get here? You're now beginning to trip out even further than us. This Westernization is reflected in the way you're having to begin to use Japanese, which is an intuitive language, as a conceptual and specific one, more like English. I'm not surprised the younger generations are suffering an identity crisis. And what is the greedy child of the agrarian and industrial revolutions? Consumerism."

I was about to put the spurs to the flanks of this exposition when Masako said, "I don't think they know what acid means," with a note of exasperation in her voice. "I can't interpret it." There was suddenly a silence and we were all staring into focusless distances around the stove—like people at a séance, waiting for a communication from the spirit world.

Mr. Nagao looked down at the wooden edge of the

hearth with an empty expression on his face, as if staring into a stream. "True. You really told me an important thing. I totally understood what you said. But if I told my children what we're talking about here, they wouldn't understand at all. You see, they think it's all old fashioned," he laughed into his reflection. "Whenever I tell them to preserve our traditions, not to copy city people, they say 'Old man, you are old fashioned. The present society is such and such.' I don't know if I can call this their resistance or what, but I believe the same as you, Mr. Ritchie, who's come from a foreign country.

"Our generation still knows how to cook rice and boil water for the bath by burning logs," he suddenly looked angry, "but the young generation under forty years of age says that science is right and that everything is becoming computerized and controlled by pressing a button. Frankly, we can't turn back, I mean the young people can't turn back. So our life in the village becomes very difficult. Soon we won't have to move—we'll do everything with a button." He was thrusting his arm into the air, with its loaded elbow firing away, and the saké and his emotions were making his face blaze with their fire. I was grazing on the verge where English and Japanese were beginning to merge into a new language.

He stabbed at the future with another cigarette. "Gradually, our old ways are disappearing. Influenced by television, we try to change our life to Western culture, for example, our houses, the way of building our houses . . ."

The *karakami* was rattling. We all looked toward it. Suddenly it opened and Mr. Nagao's wife, who had been packing *kabura-zushi* (layers of pickle turnip and salted mackerel) in a shed down the road while we had been drinking and talking, came in carrying a salted-evening-air aura about her body. She and the other village women had developed *kabura-zushi* to a fine art and turned it into a lucrative business, selling it locally as well as to other parts of Japan. The previous year they had made eight million yen and gained support from the local council to build a small pickling factory in the village.

"It's very cold today. Here's your change," she handed Masako the money with some *kabura-zushi* we had ordered.

The tension broken, after another cup and a conversation that swept the wilder shores of impossible utopias, we said goodbye. The sky was clear and some late-night kites were playing with the moon. As we left Mr. and Mrs. Nagao and Mr. Kakuma in the road, the manager of the farmers' co-op ran up to us with a calendar for the new year. Turning to bow to him, I saw Mr. Nagao beyond his shoulder, pissing beside the barn across from his house. I could see the steam rising quite plainly in the moonlight.

If you could unravel
the shadows tucked in
amongst the foliage
of the hinoki tree,
you would unwind
the calligraphy
of the year's
calendar of light.

◆ Learning About Stone Buddha Mountain

After Mr. Nagao misunderstood our inquiry about Stone Buddha Mountain and directed us to Mr. Ichigan, we finally made an appointment with Mr. Maeda, a retired primary school head teacher who lived in the village of Jindō, to which Stone Buddha Mountain is attached.

Mr. Maeda's house was a large old farmhouse with a yard and various buildings set around it. Inside the house the atmosphere and tall-ceilinged rooms reminded me of farmhouses I knew as a child in the Scottish lowlands.

Mr. Maeda met us at the *genkan* and showed us into a room with a center hearth, around which cushions had been arranged for us to sit on. The hearth itself, as was common practice, housed a large kerosene stove. At each of the hearth's four corners was placed a large, heavy glass ashtray. To my right, as I sat down, I noticed a shelf on which stood a clock, two wooden Ainu tourist carvings, the Seven Gods of Good Luck aboard a small boat, and at the end of the shelf a stuffed alligator in a glass case. High on the wall behind where Mr. Maeda sat was a very old Shintō shrine with the figure of Daikoku, a household god, enshrined. There was also a small shrine with a closed door. These objects were uniformly dark brown, having been overlaid with many winters of wood smoke from the days when the hearth was in use.

Mr. Maeda looked to be in his late sixties or early seventies. He wore heavy rimmed spectacles with clear plastic on the lower half of the frames. While speaking, a smile played around his lips, but when silent or listening to our questions his countenance assumed a stern school-teacherish expression, which I imagined could have intimidated many an unruly class into order. While he was talking, he gently rubbed one loosely fisted hand around the cupped palm of its companion, like a mortar and pestle. First the right hand in the left, then after a while the opposite arrangement as he proceeded upon his exposition.

It was not easy for him to get started at first, and there was a prelude of silence as we sat around the stove. I initiated the conversation by telling him that after discovering Stone Buddha Mountain by accident, we had found a newspaper article about it the following year and that it had aroused our curiosity. I also described some of the sites in Britain where there were standing stones and stone circles and some of the theories concerning the alignments of such places.

Placing his right fist into his left palm, he began to

grind the various ingredients of his story about Stone
Buddha Mountain. What he had to say was not apparently ordered by habit or conscious structure, as one might
expect from someone who had spent his life as a teacher,
but rather was expressed as things occurred to him, or as
one piece of information or our questioning led him from
one subject to another.

"The name of this village is Jindō (the way of the
god)," he began, pouring some hot water into a small
teapot as he spoke, then lining up three tea bowls while
the green tea briefly steeped. He poured the tea and
offered us some traditional sweets from a lacquered
wooden bowl.

"On this mountain there are two important large
stones. One is on the upper part of the mountain and the
other is just below it. They are both very interesting
stones. The lower stone is called *maedachi* ["front standing"], and it is where we hold the ritual. The upper stone
is called *okudachi* ["innermost standing"]. Just below *okudachi* there is a small group of stones, and this area is
called *karato* [a word that means a classical Chinese-style
door]. The two large standing stones are more or less the
same size. The name of the mountain is Kekkaisan [this
name indicates that it is a sacred mountain, access to
which is restricted to the practicers of the specific auster-
ities and rituals connected with the mountain], but we
call it Oyama [a respectful way of saying "the mountain"].

"The names of the kami of this mountain are
Sukunabikona no Kami, represented by the *maedachi*
stone, and Onamuchi no Mikoto, represented by the *okudachi* stone. Sukunabikona no Kami is the son of one of
the three kami that created these islands. He is small, fast
to act, has endless patience, and helped Onamuchi no
Mikoto in developing these lands. He was also the creator
of medicines and talismans. Onamuchi no Mikoto is the
son of the younger brother of Amaterasu Ōmikami, the

kami of Izumo in mythological times. Sukunabikona no Kami is the kami of agriculture. In other words, he is responsible for the building of this nation.

"When a certain scholar came to examine the stones, he said that the *maedachi* stone had been placed there by men, but that the *okudachi* stone had originally stood where we find it today, naturally."

"Is the *maedachi* stone local, or was it brought from some other area?" I asked, thinking of the stones at some of the sites in Europe.

"The scholar said that both the stones came from this mountain. There are many stones on the mountain. I imagine that the ancient people chose the biggest stone to place there."

"Is it true that no women are admitted onto the mountain?" Masako asked.

"That's right." He changed his hands over, loosely clenching his left hand and rolling it in the open palm of his right. "To the right side of the *maedachi* stone there is a group of stones where we also hold a ritual called *okama gyōji* ["iron pot ritual"—the "o" is honorific]. We put some water in an iron pot and place a *gohei* [a wand festooned with folded, white zigzag paper strips] beside it. A Shintō priest recites a prayer, and then we light a fire under the pot and heat the water. When the water is ready—it doesn't have to be very hot, just lukewarm is fine—we pour it over the *gohei* wand. Then we wipe our eyes with the wet paper of the *gohei*. I don't know exactly why, but it's for purification. We do this kind of thing at the beginning of the *okama gyōji*. We hold the same ritual in our village shrine, Hiyoshi Jinja. In the festivals that include this ritual, we wipe our eyes in the same way as we do on Oyama. It's rather unusual, isn't it?"

There was a silence, and I realized that the quietness between us extended into a deeper stillness that lay throughout the house. There were no sounds of domestic chores or the ubiquitous television, and I assumed that any other members of the family must have been out.

I still wanted to know more about the exclusion of women from the mountain, something that was common to all sacred mountains in Japan until recent times. "We were told the kami of Oyama doesn't approve of women. Do you know any stories connected with this? A farmer we met told us that a local lord or someone tried to take a mare up the mountain, but she became stuck between two trees and had to be brought down again."

"Well, although there's no evidence to support it, a scholar from Tokyo told me that the prohibition on women might have originated from the time that itinerant *yamabushi* priests [priests of a syncretic Shintō / Buddhist sect called Shugendō; see the glossary under *honji-sui-jaku*] began to visit Oyama. I'm not sure why women can't visit Oyama, but in our village, right up until the present day, women have never gone there. What it means is that prepubescent girls are allowed onto the mountain, and so also are old women whose monthly matter is finished. Even so, in this village neither young girls nor old women go onto Oyama."

"We find this kind of thing in all patriarchal cultures. It's the deeply rooted male fear and jealousy of women's power, especially around menses. That's obviously a male . . ."

Before I could go further, he said, "Many scholars have visited here, and I remember one of them saying that that was the reason and that the shape of the stone is a male symbol."

"So the main function of the kami is agricultural?"

"Yes. The festival of Oyama is held on March 1 and 2, and it usually rains or snows, both of which are essential for farming."

"Do you join in the festival every year?"

"We have other festivals in our village, which are held

for the other village shrines, but in the festival of Oyama all the men participate. I mean, the heads of families. Even those who are working elsewhere come back for the festival. Except for those who are in mourning and can't take part, all the men participate. It's very important to us."

"Is there any kind of ritual after you come down from Oyama?"

"After the ritual on Oyama we have a feast at the *omodo*'s house [the house of the man in charge of organizing the festival]. This feast is also exclusively for men. The women work in the kitchen preparing the food; they must never enter the room where the feast is being held. The serving of food and saké is left to the six men on duty.

"We each take a turn to do this duty. We work a rota system based around groups of six houses. One year the heads of one group of houses will take up the duty, the following year the six from the next group of houses, and so on until we've worked through the village. Then we begin again. The head of the group is called *omodo*, and the rest of the men are called *wakido* [supporters].

"The food must be served in red lacquerware on *akazen* [small, individual red-lacquered tray-tables]. We all have them. Without them we could not take part in the group. The group selects the one to become *omodo* among themselves. In the old days there were twenty-four houses in this village, but at present there are only nineteen. That means that each must take his turn every three years."

At the time, I wondered if there was any connection between the choice and importance of the red lacquerware and the prohibition on menstruation. It is always tempting to read things into another culture in this way and often misleading, as it is in this case. Red lacquerware is *de rigueur* at all times of feasting and celebration in Japan.

"Do you think that future generations will carry on holding the festival for Oyama?"

"Yes. I don't know when the festival began, but it has been carried on for centuries, so I believe it will continue to be held in the future. It costs a lot of money. The left side of Oyama used to be terraced with rice fields and called *miyada* ["shrine rice-field"]. Now that area is covered with trees, which were planted years ago. When I was young, though, it was the responsibility of the six men who were in charge of the festival to cultivate the rice in *miyada*. We sold the harvested rice to raise money to pay for the expense of holding the festival. But these days we all pay our share of the expenses." He held out his hand for our bowls and, filling them, handed them back to us.

"In some parts of Japan," I said, replacing my brimming bowl, "the kami of the mountain is brought down to winter in a shrine in the village, and in the spring it is returned to its abode in the mountains. Do you do anything similar here?"

"No, we don't."

"In the past," I continued, "when the kami was residing in the village, one of the local women or men would become possessed by the kami, who could then be questioned in the manner of an oracle for predictions of weather, harvest, health of the community, and so forth. Was there anything of that nature connected with Oyama?" I reached for one of the sweets.

"No. As far as I know there was nothing like that. Traditionally, however, we never take knives or blades onto Oyama. Therefore, we never cut any of the trees—not even a single blade of grass."

I began to wonder if this was some expression of fear of the so-called *vagina dentata*—the devouring aspect of the feminine associated particularly with menstruation—but decided not to pursue that line of inquiry.

He changed the position of his hands again. "Today Oyama isn't a very dark place, but when I was young it was an even more heavily wooded place. Now it is comparatively light because some years ago a big typhoon hit Noto directly and blew down lots of the trees.

"This kami is really a guardian for those of us who are involved in farming. That's why we take the ceremony very seriously. We used to celebrate fifteen different festivals a year in this village, which meant two festivals a month. The same six men had to arrange them all, but five or six years ago we thought it was a bit too much and decided to reduce the number of festivals. These days we celebrate six a year.

"There used to be a big rice field above *miyada*, where we've also planted trees now. That part was called *butaida* ["stage rice-field"] and is supposed to be the site of a stage where Noh plays dedicated to the kami were performed. Beside the *butaida*, there was a *sajikibata* where the audience sat, although we call it *sanjikibata* rather than *sajikibata*. I've heard that we used to have the Noh masks in the village, but they were kept here and there, and in the end they were all lost. No evidence exists now concerning the Noh plays, except for the names of those places."

"It's fascinating to hear these things, because in Europe we have no idea, except for the vaguest hint, of what kind of rituals were performed at our sacred pre-Christian sites. One of the great differences between Christianity and Buddhism is that wherever Christianity was transmitted to a culture it usually concentrated on first wiping most of the vestiges of the indigenous religions and beliefs, particularly since Satan had become associated with the ancient earth gods and goddesses, thus demonizing Nature in the process. Whereas Buddhism, on the other hand, allowed indigenous religions to remain, and was often influenced by them and in turn had an influence on them. *Honji-suijaku* is a case in point in Japan, and there is Bon and Buddhism in Tibet, and Taoism and Buddhism in China.

"I look at Shintō and wonder if there is anything here that might reflect what took place at some of our European indigenous religions' sites of worship before the Christian cross fell and canceled them out. It's tempting to think that there might be."

He nodded, "It's traditionally said that a long time ago a *torii* was constructed for Oyama but that it collapsed as soon as it was in place. I don't know where it was placed, but that is the story. According to one of the scholars who visited here, it was that kind of thing that stopped people from trying to change anything and thus leaving it as natural as it is. That is one reason why we never take knives or blades onto Oyama."

"Is there a special kind of prayer for this kami?"

"The Shintō priest who lives in Hiyoshi shrine in Mizuho also looks after thirteen other shrines in this area. He comes and chants a prayer that is very different from those he chants at other festivals."

"On the evening of March 1, at about ten o'clock, the ritual for the festival eve begins at the house of the *omodo*. The five other assistants gather there and place a kind of tripod made from rice straw, called *sanbawara*, in the tokonoma alcove."

"How do you make a *sanbawara*?" Masako asked, putting down her tea bowl.

"We take a bundle of rice straw, divide it into three parts, and place a *gohei* on the top. The Shintō priest then comes and chants a prayer. This ceremony is called *okomori* ["seclusion"] and is a ritual for invoking the kami. All six men stay with the kami in the house for a whole day. In the old days, after the priest had chanted, the six men would stay all night as well, but these days we go home in the evening. Now only the kami stays there and goes back to Oyama the following morning."

Mr. Maeda had removed his spectacles and was holding them up in the direction of the window, peering at the lenses. Putting them back on, he said, "I forgot to tell you what we eat at the feast. The menu never varies; it's the same every year. We eat daikon radish, *buri-namasu* [raw yellowtail fish and vegetables marinated in rice vinegar], *ohira* [five kinds of simmered vegetables, e.g., carrots, burdock, etc.], rice with red beans, and miso soup. As for drinks, we are served one small bottle of saké, and we offer it to each other using our own saké cup and bottle. For example, if I served you saké, I would give you my own saké cup and pour saké from my own bottle. This is the tradition.

"In the middle of the feast we have *otowatashi*, which is a ceremony for handing over the festival duties from the current year's six men to the men chosen for the following year. First, the incumbent group brings their own red-lacquered tray-tables into the room and eat and drink saké. When they've finished, the men for the next year's duty bring in their tray-tables, and the two groups of six men sit facing and greeting each other. The group that will assume the duties the following year say 'Thank you for your great effort!' to the group who've organized the current year's festivities. They in turn reply 'We hand it over to you for next year.' At the same time, a bottle of saké is handed over, but this is to be kept for the ceremony and not for drinking. After this, the six men drink saké from another small bottle. We call this ceremony *otowatashi*.

"The river that runs past my house is called Onoyachigawa. When we go to Oyama, we walk along the bank of the river. Just below Oyama, there used to be a large stone where it was believed that Sukunabikona no Kami landed when he came up the river by boat. Before I was born, in the Meiji era [1868–1912] the stone was moved and used as a memorial for the war dead, so you can't see it anymore.

"We used to rinse our mouths out and wash our hands

with the river water before we entered Oyama. But we don't have the stone anymore and . . ." He put his head on one side and drew in air through his teeth with a hiss. "Anyway, we stopped doing it. . . ." He paused, as though about to say one thing but changed his mind and said, "I have participated in the festival since I was twenty-five years old. At that time, the tradition of washing the hands had already ceased. When we go up Oyama for the cere- mony, however, we have to wear the kimono for formal occasions with our family crest, especially if we're a shrine representative.

"We have three shrine representatives in the village. One year when I was one of them, I got ready to go up Oyama in a Western suit. An old man who saw me came up to me and said, 'You can't go up Oyama dressed like that.' And I rushed back home to change."

"I rinsed my mouth and washed my hands with water from a tank at the bottom of Oyama," I said, wondering why he had not mentioned the tank that is supplied with water run-off from the mountain.

"You probably used the collection tank for one of the houses in the village." We all laughed.

"Each year the papers write about the festival in a seasonal article, and we've had a TV company come and film it. Altogether, we're nineteen men and the priest, and I remember some years ago there were only thirteen of us because three of the families were in mourning. That year, as many as twenty journalists and photographers came to Oyama. There were more of them than there were of us!

"This festival is a very solemn occasion for us. We all know that the festival starts on the evening of March 1 and that at ten o'clock the following morning we all go up Oyama. Even so, one of us goes to each house and announces, 'The festival of Oyama will commence this evening. Please pay a visit.' Everybody knows it, but that announcement is still made."

There was the sound of someone returning to the house—bicycle tires in the yard and a door opening somewhere at the back of the house. Mr. Maeda offered us some more tea, but we both declined. Instead, I unwrapped another of the sweets.

Mr. Maeda's hands were working again, "The other five festivals in the village are celebrated at the Hiyoshi shrine. They take place in January, March, April, August, October, and November. One of these festivals is called *kakibokkō* and we dedicate persimmons [*kaki*] to the kami. From olden times this area has been famous for its production of delicious persimmons. There used to be lots of persimmon trees in the village, but years ago most of us cut them down to enlarge our rice fields, leaving only one or two trees so we still have enough to offer to the kami."

He paused and seemed to look off in the direction of the clock. "I'm sorry, but there's no real order to my talk. Is that all right for you?"

We assured him it was fine.

"There is one object that makes Oyama a very important place for us. It is a bronze mirror that was found at the stones immediately below the *ōkudachi* stone. On one side it is decorated with scattered chrysanthemums and a pair of sparrows. When we showed it to an·expert, he said it was of the Fujiwara period [794–1185] and also that it is probable that *yamabushi* visited Oyama and dedicated it to the kami.

"I don't know when it was discovered, but the story goes that when one of the village men accidentally touched one of the stones, it moved and revealed the mirror. He showed it to all the people in the village, and they decided it should be returned to its original place because it belonged to Oyama. After the war, cultural properties became a matter of importance, and the local council applied to have Oyama registered as one of the prefecture's cultural properties. We were told that some kind of evidence would be required, and we decided to submit the mirror. In 1967, Oyama was appointed by the prefecture as a cultural property. Before that, the festival was only a village festival. Now the mirror is kept by the priest, and he brings it to Oyama for the yearly ritual.

"According to some scholars, Oyama and its festival are remnants of primitive Shintō. As far as I know, the first scholar to visit Oyama was Professor Wakamori of the Tokyo University of Education, who stayed in my house at the time. Since then many archaeologists and other experts have visited and written about their own theories concerning Oyama. When the prefectural office was examining the details of Oyama, a professor from Toyama University claimed that Oyama originated in the Fujiwara period based on the bronze mirror as evidence. But the rest of the scholars emphasized a more primitive origin. Accepting the latter opinion, the authorities eventually registered it as the remnant of primitive Shintō. Those scholars told us that there were six other places where the same type of ritual is performed. Four of these places, however, have already been altered by either the erection of a *torii* or the construction of roads. They said this was the only place that had been left completely untouched and asked us to carry on preserving it as we have been by not taking any tools or anything into Oyama."

He suddenly took the kettle, which had been gently simmering on the stove, refilled the teapot, and replenished our bowls without asking this time if we wanted any more. He then replaced his hands into their former position, as though it was a mudra for storytelling. "Recently, more people have begun to visit, including women, and most of the time I'm asked to show them Oyama. I don't know if you noticed the place where there is a *shimenawa*, but that is the boundary between Oyama and the commonly owned forest. Beyond the *shimenawa* is Oyama, which means that women can't go any further. I can't take women beyond that point, therefore I usually explain the reason and suggest that they can see some of the stones from a path that runs beside Oyama. After I've left them, if they then get into Oyama it can't be helped."

Mr. Maeda suddenly got to his feet and motioned us to follow him. He led us to a small room on one side of the house. This room contained another Shintō household shrine, which I presumed related specifically to the kami of Oyama since there was a huge frame of photographs of the ritual at Oyama on the wall beside it. One of these was a beautiful black-and-white photograph taken in the 1950s, from the approximate position of the *okudachi* stone, with everyone dressed in kimonos and kneeling in a formal position on a rice-straw mat. The other photographs were more recent, and I noticed that everyone, apart from the priest and the *omodo*, was dressed simply in a jacket and trousers with an open-necked shirt, and that instead of sitting formally they were squatting. This to me seemed to indicate a slow movement away from the ceremonial reverence toward the kami—from any deep belief in the form of Shintō it represented. In spite of Mr. Maeda's optimism, I wondered how much longer Oyama would survive as more than a form of cultural lip-service and become a historical site of interest to tourists.

"We don't usually go into Oyama," he said, as we turned toward the door, "except on the day of the festival. I heard a story about a man from the next village who went into Oyama to pick sweet chestnuts. That night he tried to get up from his futon, but found that he couldn't move. The following morning he found he was able to move again, and the first thing he did was to return all the chestnuts he had picked to Oyama."

I had been about to tell him how we had gone into Oyama and about our encounter with the snake, when I suddenly felt a metaphorical finger laid upon my lips and the steam from the kettle shushing me up.

"The festival is part of our lives and we solemnly celebrate it. My family's Buddhist sect is Sōtō Zen. We belong to a temple that is generally known as Daija-dera [Temple of the Great Snake]."

"Daija-dera?" repeated Masako, looking at me.

"Yes, a long time ago, a monk killed a huge snake through the power of his chanting. The snake used to hang from the branch of a tree at the bottom of the hill where the temple now stands. It used to swallow people as they passed by. When the monk, who was traveling around the area as part of his training, came to the village and heard of the killer snake, he went to the bottom of the hill where the snake lived, weakened it with his chanting, and then killed it. In the temple there is the monk's blood-stained surplice [kesa]. It is part of the folklore of this area.

I took out my notebook. "That's very interesting. Do you think we might be able to see it?"

"I don't know. But the temple is not far from here. You can visit it."

"Is it in the village?"

"No, it's in Mizuho. The next village. The ordinary name of the temple is Tōunji."

Mr. Maeda had set our compass on course for another journey, and we thanked him enthusiastically for his own stories and for the scent of a new one as we left his house.

◆ Night Drinking

One late summer's evening, I was sitting outside with my back against the wall of the house, watching the river on that side and enjoying drinking from a cup that was originally designed for eating buckwheat noodles from, but from which I preferred to drink saké. Darkness was just beginning to take the village by stealth, percolating from the edges of the forest and filling the spaces between the houses and the places beneath the eaves. Old Man Gonsaku returned from somewhere on his bike and carefully put it away in the fire-equipment shed. He did not see me as he turned and shuffled over to his house carrying something in a white plastic bag, because darkness had already shrouded me with its camouflage. He stopped in front of the old shambling house in the yellowing glow of the lamp on the bridge and, tilting his head back, looked up at the roof. This was something he always did before entering—perhaps an instinctual ritual, like an animal before it settles in its nest, or merely as a check to see that no tiles had slipped during the day. Then he turned to his right and looked up at the darkening sky in the direction above Sora shrine and carefully stepped down the two steps to his door. Before sliding the door open, he glanced up and down the road as if he was cognizant of the brush of my gaze but could not locate the position from whence it came. The traditional sliding door had developed a problem and kept jamming, in spite of the fact that he had spent an afternoon trying to repair it—cradling it cross-legged while sitting in the road outside his house—and it still resisted his first attempts at opening it. After struggling with it for some moments he gained entry.

Emptying my cup, I went back into the house to refill it. Masako was sitting on the floor stitching one of her wall-hangings in the room next to the kitchen, with the *karakami* open to the passage, and looked up as I passed. We briefly talked about my idea for my English class the following day.

When I returned outside, the darkness had thickened and with it a certain intensity in temperature. All the heat absorbed by the fabric of the houses and the ground—tiles, clay, wood, earth, stone, concrete, and asphalt—was now radiating out into the seemingly denser atoms of the lightless air. Even a low-wattage light bulb seemed to have acquired a strength from the sun that it did not normally possess. The outside lamp over the front door had gathered its nightly multitude of insect worshipers, and the frogs and lizards were already stationed around the area, perusing the menu. Now and then, one of them would suddenly flick from its former motionless posture, with a snatch-change of position, like an autonomous chess piece on the wooden lattice on either side of the door, and the game would be checkmate for yet another bug.

A sudden movement of water made me lean forward from my place against the wall and look up-river to my right, where the water passed between an empty, unlit house on the opposite bank and the barn adjoining the back of our own house where it was impenetrably dark. There was a splash, and I slowly stood up and tried to lance the dark by narrowing my eyes, which, of course, made no sense. Once I relaxed my eyes again, an area of the dark seemed to shift, and with a familiar shriek a heron flew off, leaving the sound of a rosary of drops falling back into the river from its feet and the rhythmic sighing of its wings as it passed up among the stars.

There was silence in the village again, and the effects of the saké had stepped up my olfactory register, so that I seemed to be not only smelling the blend of the environmental cocktail one minute and differentiated levels of it the next but new stratas again within these levels. Some of these catalyzed associations and memories often seemingly not my own. They worked like olfactory mnemonics for a recall that was so powerful that part of my being seemed to be falling through a series of time shifts.

I was jolted out of these reveries by the return of Mr. and Mrs. Sakashita in their white pickup as it drew up beside their house directly across the road from ours, and to one side of the fire-equipment shed. There was a steep ramp up onto the space between the shed and the Sakashita's house, and as the small truck drove up it, there was the familiar clunk-clank as the wheels hit the iron drain-cover halfway up. This sound always announced the arrival or departure of the Sakashita's— morning, lunch time, and evening—as they went to and from their work.

Mr. and Mrs. Sakashita lived with their son who, after his graduation from university and unlike most of his col- lege-educated peers, decided to remain and work in the area at the Anamizu council offices. Mr. Sakashita senior, concerned about the difficulties faced by village people in making a living without going outside the area, had start- ed a small curtain factory in one of the several empty houses in the center of the village. This meant that, while retaining their own rice fields, he and his wife had sub- stantially increased their workload, particularly as they felt they had to be seen to work harder than their own employees (something I found common among people in the village who employed their neighbors).

The deep growl of a boat's diesel engine sounded from the quay beyond the bridge as someone set out night fishing. I returned into the house for another refill and then carried it over to the vermilion bridge. I leaned over the railings on the seaward side next to Old Man Gonsaku's house. The sound of the fishing boat was receding as it entered the open waters of the bay. I looked down into the water. There in the light from the road lamp over the bridge were hundreds, perhaps thousands, of small fish stacked in gently waving strata, heading into the flow of the incoming tide. Now and then, one of them would suddenly turn and move a stratum up or down, its silver underbelly flashing like lightning in the darkened river. I watched them, wondering if it was the light that attracted them, the mix of river and seawater at that place, or whether they grazed where the waters met.

Gently moving in toward the bridge from the darkness of the inlet beyond where the boats were moored to the quay and just entering the illuminated arena of fish was the pale moon-colored body of a dead squid. It looked like the hand of an extraterrestrial. As I watched it, a light came on in Old Man Gonsaku's kitchen and he appeared at the sink by the window in his sleeping kimono with an old faded, sleeveless jacket over it. He turned on the tap and bent over to splash water on his face, then turned off the tap and disappeared back into the interior as the window blacked out again.

As I returned my attention to the gently waving squid, there was the sound of someone trying to open the front door. After some rattling and banging, accompanied by some incoherent words of impatience, Old Man Gonsaku emerged and, without seeing me, went down the side of his house and emptied the contents of a small jar into the river. He stood looking down into the water in the shadowy light from the bridge and farted the croak of a raven.

As quietly as possible, I said, "Good evening," and he jumped. seeing me, he started to giggle. "Ah, Mr. Ritchie!" He came around onto the bridge beside me and at that moment Masako, who had observed the preceding moments, came across the road, laughing.

Old Man Gonsaku looked at my cup and I passed it to him, "Please, drink it all." He giggled and took a mouthful. We all looked down at the fish. The dead squid was now passing over them, its tentacles gently moving in the flow, making it look as though it was counting them.

I asked him how his wife was, and he said she was already in her futon. Then he began to thank us for taking her to the clinic, all over again. He tipped his head back and emptied the contents of the cup into his throat. Containing more than he realized, some of it overflowed onto his kimono. He wiped his mouth on the back of his hand. "Haaaaa . . . Thank you very much," and passed the cup back to me. Bowing and giggling, he turned on "Goodnight," and went down the steps to his house.

The door must not have opened fully when he had first come out, because when he returned through the doorway, his body struck both the jamb and the door itself. This may have been due to his not being too steady on his feet, however, after perhaps more than his nightly quota.

Masako returned to the house and I remained, listening to his movements in the interior of his house as he proceeded along the passage and up the stairs. I stayed on the bridge until I heard the dead-weight thump of his body as he dropped down into his futon.

> From the brilliant dark,
> the fragile threat
> of a cloud
> stalks the moon.

◆ The Tiger Nembutsu

It was August, with the temperature in the eighties and high humidity, the air vibrating with cicadas like molecular heat-hymns. I had left Sora to spend another period at the temple of my priest friend, Shorō Fukuda. There I took part in the daily life of a country temple in an area that is a stronghold of the Shin sect of Pure Land Buddhism.

Each morning before breakfast, I would sit behind Rev. Fukuda senior, then in his eighties, in front of the altar, where he would try to teach me to chant the *shōshinge* (Shin doctrine rendered in verse form) and the Amida Sutra. He had his own style and rhythm of chanting which always left me straggling behind and lost after a very short time. Once I had lost my place, because of my slowness in reading the script, I could only sit and listen to him chanting. The sound of his voice and the shaping of the chant came from his body in the way the chant of a stream is articulated by its stones, and the stones themselves are shaped by the chant. These sounds had echoed in his body since he was a child and now flowed out without artifice or effort.

After the service, he would turn to me and with great patience explain some point or other about whatever he had been—and I should have been—chanting, partly in Japanese, but occasionally switching to English when the words presented themselves to him.

While I was there, I was fortunate to be given the opportunity to attend a study group conducted by an eminent scholar-priest, Rev. Ryūshin Uryūzū, who lived in a nearby village. The studies served to deepen and expand the knowledge of the area's priests. During my attendance, he very generously taught the classes in both Japanese and English. The deep impression this kindness made on me has remained with me ever since.

My days were occupied with morning and evening services, reading some unpublished manuscripts on Shin Buddhism written in English by another eminent scholar-priest who had only recently died, study groups and temple meetings organized by Shorō, and sudden unannounced excursions that he had to make to other nearby temples or to show me places he thought would be of interest to me.

One day he announced we were going to visit Saifukuji temple on the island of Okinoshima in Lake Biwa. He wanted to show me the "Tiger Nembutsu," a scroll bearing the Nembutsu in the calligraphy of the great Shin monk Rennyo, who reformed the Shin sect [Jōdo Shinshū] in the fifteenth century and brought it to the prominent position it holds today, as the largest sect in Japan.

After driving to a small harbor where we met up with a group of ten or so women from the congregation of his temple, we crossed over the water to the island by fishing boat. It was another beautiful and very hot day as we walked through the small fishing village and up to the temple. The priest's wife was there to meet us and led us into a specially built annex. It was here that the "Tiger Nembutsu" was enshrined. The priest's wife told us the story connected with it. While the Shin sect generally eschews the supernatural, there are nevertheless many such stories associated with it, including at least one connected with its founder, Shinran. Here is the story she told:

On the island of Okinoshima in the fifteenth century there lived a man called Juemon, whose wife died in childbirth. But her spirit could not rest and thus appeared each night in its eagerness to see the child. Feeling great compassion for it, Juemon wanted to seek the advice of an enlightened priest. Strangely, one night the tutelary kami of the place appeared to him in a dream and said, "Tomorrow a boat will come to this island and on it will be the great monk Rennyo. Go to see him immediately and receive his teaching."

It happened that at that time Rennyo was traveling from Yoshizaki in Echizen (present-day Fukui prefecture) to Jikyōji temple (in Shiga prefecture) when a storm blew up and the ship he was on had to seek shelter in Okinoshima.

When Juemon saw the ship, he rushed down to the quay where he met Rennyo and told him about his dream. Rennyo said, "I understand," and followed Juemon back to his house, where Juemon then told him about the visitations from the spirit of his dead wife.

Rennyo stayed at Juemon's house that night, and when the spirit of Juemon's wife appeared, Rennyo taught her spirit the *tariki hongan* (the primal vow of other power). He counseled her spirit to believe in Amida Buddha and to wholeheartedly say the *nembutsu*. But her spirit replied, "I deeply appreciate your teachings, but I can't say the *nembutsu*, owing to my sinful acts."

Listening to the spirit, Rennyo felt even deeper compassion for her. Taking a piece of paper and a brush and inkstone, he laid the paper on a rice-straw mat and wrote out the six-character *nembutsu*—Namu Amida Butsu. When it had dried he gave it to the spirit, who accepted it with gratitude and disappeared "like a candle being blown out."

The following night the spirit reappeared in front of Juemon, holding the paper with the *nembutsu* written on it in her hand, and said, "Because of the sacred teachings of the great monk, I could be born in Amida's Pure Land and be liberated from eons of suffering. I want to give this *nembutsu* to my child." And her spirit handed it to Juemon, with a cloth on which to mount it as a scroll, and then disappeared forever.

The next day Juemon asked Rennyo, "What is the power of the primal vow?" and Rennyo taught him the doctrine of *shinjin* (immediate entry into the Pure Land as an ordinary sinful being). Juemon was deeply moved and overwhelmed with gratitude toward Rennyo and immediately had his head shaved and became his disciple, with the Buddhist name of Sairyō.

Before Rennyo left to continue his voyage, he wrote four lines from the *shōshinge* and gave them to Sairyō. These are enshrined at Saikufuji temple with the "Tiger Nembutsu." Where he had laid the paper on the rice-straw mat, the pressure of the brush on the paper had picked up the impression of the woven lines in the straw through the ink, resulting in a striped effect, hence giving this written *nembutsu* its name, "Tiger Nembutsu."

> Nembutsu—
> *even in the brief*
> *breath of a gnat*
> *on a bent blade of grass*

♦ *Temple of the Great Snake*

I was very keen to follow up on Mr. Maeda's story about Tōunji temple (or Daija-dera) and find out more about the giant snake and if possible see the blood-stained *kesa* (surplice).

Masako phoned the temple and spoke to the priest, the Rev. Mitsuo Fujitate, who explained to her that the temple belonged to the Sōtō Zen sect and gave her directions from the village of Mizuho. He suggested we visit on the following Wednesday afternoon.

At the village of Mizuho, we turned off the main road onto a single track that led up through the trees of a small forested mountain. At the top, the road stopped in front of an image of Jizō and a flight of stone steps that led up to the temple. To the left of the Jizō was the temple graveyard.

It was a warm autumn afternoon, and crickets scratched dryly in the yellow grasses as we walked up the steps. The temple stood guarded by large cedars beyond the huge sweep of its roof. Rev. Fujitate greeted us at the door and led us through to a tatami room in the living quarters of the temple. It was a large, tall-ceilinged room with an old nineteenth-century wall clock and a Shintō household shrine. He invited us to sit at a table with a plate of rice crackers at its center.

He looked to be in his mid- to late-thirties and wore a monk's working clothes—blue-cotton collarless jacket with tie fastening and baggy pants. As we found so often in the initial stages of these kinds of interviews, it took him some time to speak, and he busied himself making tea. We sat in a silence that rode the late afternoon shadows through the window, as they became stretched by the clock's hands.

We drank some tea, and I asked again what sect the temple was affiliated to, since I wished to verify that it was indeed the Sōtō Zen sect. My reason for this was that the story of the snake Mr. Maeda had told us was much more the kind of lore associated with temples of the two Tantric sects, Shingon or Tendai, rather than with a Zen temple. I wondered if the temple's affiliation had changed at some time during its history, as is common, but he insisted that it had always been a Zen temple. "This temple was founded in 1398 by a monk called Mutsugai Shōō, and I'm the thirty-second generation. It has always been a Zen temple."

"Can you tell us about the snake?"

"Well, the story goes that there was a huge poisonous snake living in a pond just below where this temple now stands. It used to cause damage to the crops by creating storms and it also used to threaten and kill passersby, so the village naturally lived in great fear of it.

"One day, a monk called Mutsugai Shōō was passing through the village on his begging rounds when he heard the terrible story of the snake. Well, he felt very sorry for the villagers and decided to do something about it, he chanted and prayed for seven days and nights until the pond where the snake lived dried out. Then Mutsugai Shōō fought with the snake and killed it. Everyone was very happy to be rid of the snake, and the whole village prospered again. The local lord was so pleased that he gave Mutsugai Shōō this land on which to build a temple.

"In this temple here, we have Mutsugai Shōō's bloodstained *kesa* and a bone from the snake. We also have a document signed by the local lord offering this site for the temple. These are the temple's three treasures."

"Would it be possible for us to see them?" I asked eagerly.

He scratched his head, "No, I'm sorry. They're displayed to the public only every seven years. That is the tradition. There's a village song, though, that tells the story. I'll write it out for you. He took a piece of paper from beneath what looked like a pile of documents beside him and started to write the story down in pencil, bending over the table while we munched on rice crackers. When he finished, he handed it to us.

Then he got to his feet, "Come, I'll show you the snake's grave."

We followed him out of the temple and into the warm late afternoon air. He led us to the edge of the compound, where it overlooked a kind of hollow. There were rice fields that had obviously been abandoned for many years. "That's where the snake's pond used to be," he said, pointing at it. "There used to be a giant cedar tree beside the road just down there called *daijasugi* [big-snake cedar]. That was where the snake used to wait to attack passersby, but it was blown down by a typhoon some years ago."

He turned and walked past the main Buddha Hall and up the rising ground behind the temple on a small, narrow path that led in a direction where I could see farther on some graves on a bank to one side of the path.

Looking back toward us, he said, "The bones of the snake, after it was killed, were collected by the villagers. They crushed the bones when they were needed to be used as medicine. There was a story that some of them had been buried in a pot underneath the Jizō image where you parked your car, but when we had it renovated recently we found a pot but no bones."

We had now reached the graves. There were three. "This is the grave of Mitsugai Shōō," he said pointing at a headstone in the middle. "On the right is the grave of the local lord. And here to the left is the grave of the snake."

There was a pleasing symmetry in the alignment of the three graves of the protagonists in this fascinating story, all united and equal in their remains. The snake buried in the temple of the village it had terrorized, and the lord who had honored the one who had killed it—the itinerant monk, the hero himself, who had been the snake's executioner, buried between them.

I took a photograph of the graves and asked Rev. Fujitate if he minded me taking a picture of him, in case the book I wanted to write was published. We then left a small gift we had brought with us on the table in his room and said goodbye. He stood waving at the top of the temple steps as we drove back down the mountain.

This kind of story is very common as an allegory or symbolic tale of the capping, or controlling, of an elemental energy of some kind, or of the converting, transmuting, or purifying of some base energy or lower level of consciousness (in myths, the symbology of spiritual evolution, etc.), but here the evidence suggests an actual event. I heard of a similar story connected with another temple in the area featuring a giant crab that was killed by a monk, who then founded a temple on the site.

This is a rough translation of a Mizuho village song:

The Killing of the Great Snake of Mizuho
Here, in Yamada, a pond
Was the most dangerous place in Noto.
It was the home of a huge,
Formidable and venomous snake.

Passersby tried to escape it
By hiding in the grass beside the pond,
Where a girl had searched for her father,
Who had already been taken by the snake.

A traveling monk, all the way from Enshu
Passed through the village one day,
And on hearing of their terrible plight
Determined to ask Buddha's help in killing the snake.

Fulfilling his vow to chant for seven days and nights,
His prayers were answered,
And the snake became sickly and weak,
And he killed it with one stroke of a sword.

The empty pond filled up with its blood,
And life returned to the village once more.
In appreciation for the monk's great work,
Lord Tomura Shūji built him a temple.

The village has five hundred years of history,
And the wind from Futago Mountain
Still tells the old story in the ancient cedar
In which the snake used to rest.

Here is a type of Buddhist chant called a *go-eika*, which is a poem or song usually chanted by women. Below is one chanted by a women's group in Tōunji temple, only here the pond has become a cave, but with a very nice water image that carries the motif of transformation:

> *Destroyed a cave*
> *That had been the dwelling*
> *Of a venomous snake,*
> *So that from it came*
> *A mountain stream of*
> *Buddha's sweet water.*

This is a children's song from Mizuho village, quite unrelated to the story of the snake. It was sung to us by Mrs. Kitayama, the wife of the headman of Sora, who was born in Mizuho and sang it herself as a child. It describes the identifying features of three monks in the locality, who, as is common, are called by the names of their temples, ending with Tōunji:

The monk with the smooth, bald head
— that's Taisenji.

The monk who's very short
— Seianji.

The monk with round eyes
— Tounji.

◆ Preparing Goodbye and "The Straight Path of Sincerity"

Our neighbor, Yukiko, was standing in our kitchen. She looked even smaller indoors, as she laid the vegetables she had brought us from her vegetable patch on the kitchen table. As I watched her, I suddenly felt that this was the moment we should tell her that we were going to have to leave and return to Britain. Masako began slowly to tell her the reasons why we could not stay any longer in Sora. Yukiko's face at first was filled with the usual attentive interest, bordered with the flickering suggestion of a torrent of giggles waiting in the corners of her body, when it suddenly changed, like the light on a field when a cloud passes over the sun. It became taut and troubled, and while her body suddenly froze her left hand seemed to fumble, in an autonomy of panic for the corner of her sleeveless jacket. The focus in her eyes seemed to have lost Masako's face and began staring off into the distance far beyond her. Then her dear, toothless old mouth began to work and a fractured cry went up from it, *"Sabishii! Sabishii!"* ("Lonely! Lonely!") She lifted the corner of her jacket to the glinting tears that fell down her cheeks. She continued to cry *"Sabishii! Sabishii!"* till the energy that charged the word penetrated our own hearts and the same tears streamed down our faces. *"Sabishii"* echoed deeper and deeper, till we stood like this for some minutes, stripped of our ages, our cultures, and each on the same spot, sharing the same shadow in the dim light from the kitchen window.

She sobbed down the passageway to the *genkan*. We tried to console her, and our own hearts, by saying that we would be remaining for a while yet and, anyway, we would return. As she turned toward us, beyond the *genkan* step, a smile seemed to struggle against the stiff salted skin of her cheeks, and the dark, empty interior of her mouth sharply defined the boundaries of her lips as the muscles in her face seemed to come in conflict with each other and produce a complex and confused grin.

According to the traditional, conventional etiquette of village life, the first person to be informed of our decision to leave should have been the headman. It was only through first visiting the headman, and holding a meeting, that we were allowed permission to live within the community in the first place, so it seemed perfectly natural that we should carry out the taking of our leave in the same fashion. Now that we had told Yukiko, we knew we should waste no time in informing Mr. Sakashita, who had only recently assumed the role of headman from Mr. Kitayama.

A few days later, we called on Mr. Sakashita fairly late in the evening in order to give him time to have returned from his curtain factory, taken a bath, and had his dinner. We were met at the door by Mrs. Sakashita, who showed us through to the guest room where Mr. Sakashita was sitting in a *nemaki* (light cotton sleeping kimono) with a top jacket, drinking and smoking with his son Toshihiko and a small dapper man wearing a black suit, who, with his dark swarthy skin and short stature, reminded me of a Cornishman or a Pictish man like my grandfather. It was obvious that they were already quite drunk, and they hailed us loudly, making space for us on the tatami around a table at the center of the room. As Mrs.

Sakashita poured saké for us, and the men shouted and laughed, I noticed an expression on her face that was one I had seen on many occasions on the faces of village women. It is an expression borne of impatience that has been transmuted through discipline over the years and bears at least the external appearance of calm resignation and tolerance. I suspect, though, that it is probably a behavioral life raft, which is clung to when circumstances threaten to emotionally swamp the situation.

Mr. Sakashita introduced the small dark man as his cousin, Mr. Kawakami, who lived behind our house and whom I had failed to recognize in his suit. As we sat drinking, we told Mr. Sakashita the reason for our visit.

"Oh, but we were just talking about you the other evening. We decided to give you a rice field. Why do you want to go back?"

We explained the reasons why it was necessary to return at this time, but that we would come back in the future to see them. They listened to our reasons, nodding and exhaling dense fogs of smoke into the center of the room.

Later, while the saké was having its wondrous way with my senses and Mr. Kawakami was explaining something to me that I did not understand, Mr. Sakashita called excitedly to me from an adjoining room, the *karakami* to which was open. I allowed Mr. Kawakami to finish his incomprehensible exposition and then entered the next room.

"Look at this, Mr. Ritchie! I want to know what you think of this." He drew me in front of the tokonoma alcove, where his son and wife and Masako were already kneeling. There hanging in the tokonoma was a scroll of extraordinary, vigorous calligraphy that dashed and swirled with the energy of lightning bolts striking through a wild, torrential waterfall. Though its effect may well have been heightened by the saké, it was nevertheless exhilarating, like the contained forces of some ideographic storm.

I told him how wonderful it was and expressed my admiration of it, though I could in no way decipher its meaning, as is often the case with that kind of calligraphy, even for Japanese. "My uncle did that. He was a very gifted calligrapher. Do you know what he wrote it with?" I shook my head, expecting him to say something outlandish like the neighbor's cat or a bunch of daikon leaves, saké filling me with all kinds of similar expectations. "I didn't have a large enough brush in the house at the time, so he grabbed a handful of maybe six or seven brushes in a bundle, like this," he made a fist as though grasping something and then made a kind of stirring motion over the tatami.

I was still sitting hypnotized by the racing ink, when I heard Mr. Sakashita's voice speaking excitedly somewhere, some distance to my right, "Look at this, Mr. Ritchie! You're interested in Buddhism, aren't you? Come and look at this." He had moved over to the Buddhist altar that was in the right end of the same wall as the tokonoma. The doors had been closed after evening chanting, and he began to open them, helped by his wife, as he was now a little unsteady, even while sitting down. "Look at this. It's very old. He reached into the main altar in the center and, grasping hold of the Buddha image there, pulled it out.

"Careful father, you'll break it," frowned Toshihiko.

"Look at that," he thrust the image into my hands. It was carved of wood and was obviously of quite some age. I told him what a beautiful image it was. "Yes," he said, and getting up on his knees to put it back on the altar, he fell into the altar. Both his wife and his son shouted at him and struggled to pull him out, complaining and castigating him. The image was not standing properly, so he leaned forward and tried to correct its position. As he did so, part of the image fell off. Toshihiko took the image from him and almost fell into the altar himself. Once the image was back on the altar, Mrs. Sakashita very firmly closed the doors herself, by which time, Mr. Sakashita had moved to another part of the room and was already rummaging through a cupboard.

"I want to give you something," he said into the depths of the cupboard. Then he started pulling out long boxes that looked as though they contained scrolls. After taking the lids off several of them and half unrolling the scrolls, leaving his wife and son to roll them up again, and overtaking their efforts to clear up by pulling yet more out and strewing them all over the floor, he let out a yell of triumph, "Here it is! I want you to have this."

He laid the scroll on the tatami and with sudden, apparently complete control and concentration, he very carefully unrolled it bit by bit. It was beautiful. The ink fused with the same dynamic energy possessed by the calligraphy scroll in the tokonoma, and was obviously by the same hand. "My uncle did this, too. I want you to have it and take it back to Britain."

"But Mr. Sakashita, it's wonderful, but I don't know that we can accept it. You must treasure it very much. What does it say?"

He followed the swirling strokes with a finger, which looked as if it had been taken over by the energy of the ink's current. "Sincerity . . . Straight . . . Path," he said, and looked up, his face shining with emotion and saké.

I awoke somewhere in the night and worried slightly that Mr. Sakashita might suffer alcoholic amnesia, having bestowed on us such an extraordinary gift, and that that block might suddenly be breached while he was involved in some trivial domestic chore, with a sudden wrenching shock of regret. But I sensed just before falling over into sleep again that this thought was not worthy of either the gift or the occasion.

◆ Burning Cedar, the Waterfall Kami, and a High Fever

Having packed our few belongings and sending them for shipping back to Britain, we moved into the temple for a short time. One morning very early, causing us to scramble out of the futon, an old woman called Mrs. Sumi Takiya, from whom we regularly bought vegetables, that she wheeled around the village on a barrow, came into the *genkan*. There was a very strong wind coming off the sea, and she said that she found it too difficult to walk back home against it. She wore a waterproof coat, with a hood over the hand towel she always wore tied around her head, winter or summer. She had the beautiful, open face of a Buddhist nun. We invited her to sit and warm herself while we made her a pot of green tea and prepared breakfast for ourselves.

As we sat down, she said, "I was so sad when I heard the Tanis were moving from this temple to Jifukuin temple in Nakai. Senjuin is not my temple, but from time to time I visit to worship, and whenever the temple had big gatherings I helped Chisato [Mrs. Tani] with the cooking."

In fact, Mrs. Takiya's own cooking was delicious, and she often sold her cooked vegetables, seaweed, and shellfish house-to-house in the village. During the winter, she also knitted woolen hats and sold them very cheaply, because most old people wear hats in the house during the winter due to the coldness of the rooms.

"Did you know," she continued, looking into her cup and turning it slowly on its lacquered coaster, "that Chisato dreamed that Miroku Bosatsu [Maitreya, the Buddha of Tomorrow—the image enshrined at Jifukuin temple] appeared and said, 'You should restore Jifukuin temple and help revive the village.'" We shook our heads. "Well, at about the same time three years ago, the cedars in front of the Buddha hall of Jifukuin temple were blown down in a storm, as if to show them where to build their house. Of course, that is where they've built it.

There was a short discussion about the differences between the two temples and how busy Rev. Tani was going to be, having to attend to two congregations. "Someone said you had been asking about the waterfall near Mr. Muroki's house." (The one where we found the remains of a shrine.) We nodded. "Well, I wanted to tell you a story about it before you leave. Mr. Michishita's mother could heal sickness. She told me that Kōbō Daishi [founder of the Shingon sect] appeared in a dream and told her he would help her to heal people. That was why she began to help sick people. I knew a child who was crippled and couldn't walk, but could walk again after being healed by her."

The fingers of her right hand were curled around her cup while the left hand rested on the table. A fly had landed on this hand and was examining the middle knuckle of the third, or ring, finger. It seemed to have found something of interest in one of the creases there. As she moved it flew off, making two or three low passes over our empty dishes before moving to some other part of the room.

"When my son got sick with a high fever that old woman said to me, 'You burned the branches of a cedar tree at the shrine of the waterfall didn't you?' I said, 'Yes.' She said, 'That's why he's got a fever. You must go and beg the kami's pardon. You mustn't behave without due respect. Take saké to the shrine and sprinkle it over the ground and beg the kami's pardon.' I did what she said, and when I got home my son's fever had gone.

"One day she said, 'I'll teach you something. This is only for you, no one else. When you get sick, write *onko-rokoro sendani mawasoka* three times on the palm of your hand with your finger and blow on it three times. Then you will get well.' That old woman told me that I would be reborn into a temple family when I die."

She finished her tea. "When I went to Iwakuraji temple, I met a man who was also visiting the temple. He said to me, 'These days, people have lost *shinjin* [the true realization of Amida Buddha's compassion active throughout the universe]. When I meet people of deep *shinjin*, words just come out of my mouth one after another. But when I come face to face with people of no faith, no words come out at all.'"

By the time Mrs. Takiya arose to leave, the wind had dropped marginally and she decided to walk back to her house.

A lot of people will find the burning cedar story quaint nonsense, but I believe it is much more than that. Many belief systems teach an understanding of the phenomenal universe, describing it as an energetic process characterized by interdependency and manifesting itself at many different vibratory levels and in which, fundamentally, there is no actual separation between ourselves and the environment "in" which we live. In fact, in a true sense we are that environment—an environment that is both intelligent and sacred in nature. Even in our dualistic relationship with it, there is a direct correspondence between our attitudes and actions toward it and the effect those actions and attitudes have on ourselves. (This is only too tragically obvious in terms of the environmental damage we have already wrought and the dire consequences thereof.) This being the case, then might not this story be teaching us something of the greatest importance in the relationship between the burning of the kami's cedar and the burner's child suffering a high temperature.

We have forgotten how to ask permission of Nature, as we have forgotten gratitude for what we still are in the habit of calling "Nature's gifts"—which in fact we actually steal—which we have made in reality "spoils." How do we behave at the shrine that is this planet? What kind of burning have we been doing? And what kind of high fever may our children expect in global warming? No, this simple story carries a vitally important message and warning. And poses the all important question—how on Earth are we going to beg this planet's pardon?

> *Already*
> *summer's flown—*
> *the wings*
> *of dead bugs*
> *litter*
> *the windowsill.*

◆ A Village of Autumn

It was autumn again. The stubble in the drained rice fields was burning, filling the village with the incense of the earth and the forest with the ethereal mists of the burning corpse of summer. Women sat in groups by the sides of the fields after their work, their laughter as it reached across the stubble intermittently punctuated by the cry of a circling kite, like an old brown kimono hanging on the sky as if it, too, were scorched by autumn's favor.

I looked across at the old wood and clay houses of the village under their dark tiles, down the road to my right. In the low sun, they glowed gold, yellow, and brown, their weathered cedar, charcoal gray, as though they burned inwardly at the heart of each atom of their composition. Everything seemed to be burning in a radiant elegiac light. And as the smoke suddenly turned, I momentarily saw the village as a ghost, the smoke like wind through an empty gown—what had been of substance, a residual image lingering on the rim of Time's event horizon. And the acidity in the smoke made my eyes smart and water, showing me the appropriate response.

I tried to imagine that a spring would follow the winter already telegramed in the eyes and movements of our neighbors, the exposed bamboo lathes and missing tiles, and the weed-choked fields that encroached on Sora and the neighboring villages. I fantasized unseen seeds, that the village would survive or as though the present inhabitants were somehow immortals, already inhabiting some kind of timeless space. But it was only a dream and nonsense and quickly exorcised by the steepening shadow from the forest at my back.

I got up from where I had been sitting and walked through the village and beyond by the shore road. As I walked, I became surrounded by a host of red dragonflies, which symbolize autumn to the Japanese. They accompanied me all the way, flashing in the low-angled light as they zigzagged, diving and swooping. I felt like a ship escorted by dolphins, and I knew that my compass was already set on course for the return journey to Britain.

When I finally reentered the village, the air was already blue with dusk and the perfumed smoke from the bathhouse fires. In the room with the Buddhist altar there was a vase in front of the image containing a single, wild mountain lily. Its scent filled the room, as though it had just been vacated by a celestial being.

> The dead cicada
> has stored her song
> deep in the heart
> of the hinoki tree.

◆ Afterword ◆

As a child at a boarding school in the wilds of the Scottish lowlands, there was a tree that I adopted as confidante and friend. And it was to this tree that I entrusted my own most-secret thoughts and fears. At this time, too, wandering in the forests and wild places around the school, I frequently became immersed in a kind of intoxicating and bewitching fugue, augmented by what, even at the early and innocent ages between six and ten, I imagined to be the scent of the power and energy of the sex of trees and grasses—the immanence of something in the natural world in which I found myself that I could neither describe nor give form to through imagery or words.

It was while living in Sora that I found a return to these early experiences of mystery and awe, in a similar kind of intimate rapport, at both a primitive and spiritually sophisticated level, in the culture and lives of the old people of the Noto Peninsula. It was their innocent trust in and reverence toward the natural environment, their relationship with it, and daily expressions of gratitude toward it for what they received, whether it was what they wanted or not, that constantly moved and inspired me, often at unexpected moments. In fact, in the case of two women we knew, this gratitude and their faith in the kami and Buddha was such that, though each suffered a terminal illness, they were able to express thanks for their condition—such was their humble, open-hearted-and-minded acceptance and undemanding trust in life.

In places in this book, I have briefly described something of what I understand to be the real meaning of culture, and the denial and ignorance of that meaning in our present cultural condition in the West. It was my experience of living amongst the elders of Sora that both heightened this awareness and at the same time filled me with a feeling of deep mourning, by offering me a glimpse of how things had been and were now fast ceasing to be, on the very peninsula on which I was living at the time.

Japan has always been a kind of cultural oyster. While actually creating little of originality, with a few notable exceptions, from within the boundaries of its own coastlines, it took in grit from other cultures, chiefly mainland China and the Korean peninsula, which it then refashioned and modified into its own cultural pearls. Having closed its doors to all outside cultural influences in the mid-seventeenth century for over two hundred years, when it finally reopened them, it was to look exclusively to the West for what it saw as new cultural sustenance. The grit it enthusiastically ingested from the perceived superior West, however, has resulted, as I have said elsewhere in this book, in the demise of its own profound culture. What it took in from the West, I believe, were cultural carcinogens, which have destroyed the pearls it had taken centuries to produce and are fast reducing Japan culturally and spiritually to an empty shell. The postwar American Occupation and its attendant victor/vanquished psychology obviously further deepened this cultural wound.

Japan, as it had always done in the past, improved upon what it absorbed and made it its own, until it has become the leading technological/consumer society in the world. Ironically, on the world trading scene it is included among the Western trading economies. It has even progressively and voraciously been destroying the natural environment with which it once identified and understood as sacred, in order to feed this insatiable appetite and with it its own spiritual heritage. A similar scenario is now being repeated with the remaining cultures of Asia—at least those that have not yet been, or are not in the process of being, destroyed by the ravages of totalitarianism. A catastrophe every bit as serious as deforestation—the removal of ecological lungs—only here it is the collapsing of the organs of spiritual breath.

If these Oriental countries who have sold their birthrights for the hot message of consumerism were to look back, they would find no path that has led them to the place they now find themselves. That is to say, they have arrived at the devouring edge of consumerism without any cultural process. They have arrived like someone taking LSD or traveling by jet. They don't know how they got there. Their collective disorientation and confusion must therefore be all the greater.

An important indicator of the damage Japan has done itself is in the replacement of the word *"jinen"* with the word *"shizen."* While the original Chinese characters remain the same, the pronunciation and meaning have altered. The former nondualistic word *"jinen"* means what we call "Nature" or "the environment," Buddha, the kami, and humankind, *as part of* a holistic continuum. The latter conceptual, dualistic, and objective word *"shizen"* was introduced into the Japanese language to replace *"jinen"* due to the influence of Western dualistic philosophical thought, meaning as it does "Nature" or "the environment" *as apart from* humankind—a "Fall" that Japan has allowed to be visited upon itself.

To look back longingly at the past of a once profound and noble culture and mourn its passing is not, I believe, to indulge in nostalgia or sentimentality, nor to imagine a utopia—that would be nonsense—but rather to suffer a terrible feeling of loss, and the fact that that loss is not being replaced by anything equally or more meaningful. It is to recognize the deepening impoverishment of the human spirit.

In Buddhist eschatology, there is a transient after-life hell-state called the Realm of Hungry Ghosts (all the Buddhist after-death realms reflect psychological and spiritual conditions and are by their natures transient), in which the inhabitants have monstrously huge bodies, but tiny mouths, and suffer insatiable appetites that they can never satisfy. This is an acutely accurate picture of consumerism. Consumerism (the Big "C" of materialism) has consumed the human spirit. We have spiritually died and already live in the Realm of Hungry Ghosts.

The Japanese seem to have forgotten what they once knew, essentially, without having to think about it, that the land, the environment, is the body of Buddha, the body of the kami, and is also essentially their own body. As I have said above, it is now autumn in the rural villages of Japan, but one without any potential for renewal, with all the consequences for what remains of its cultural heart and mind. It is an autumn, or as Americans say, "fall," in which we all share the blame and the consequences.

◆ Glossary ◆

Ainu: The aboriginal race of the Japanese archipelago.

Bashō: Japan's most famous haiku poet (1644–94). Formed his own school of poetry, influenced by Zen Buddhism.

Bodhisattva: Whereas the Theravada school is mainly concerned with individual liberation, the Mahayana school is altruistic in outlook and concerned with the liberation of all sentient beings. Nothing expresses this ideal more powerfully than the bodhisattva principle, in which a being who has reached the state of spiritual maturity necessary for the attainment of supreme enlightenment (Nirvana) postpones his or her final liberation in order to continue reincarnating to help all other beings to recognize the path to Buddhahood.

Archetypically, bodhisattvas represent different attributes of Buddha (the Absolute), e.g., wisdom, compassion, etc.

Buddhism: The core of the historical Buddha, Sakyamuni's enlightenment, lies in the realization that the ego-self that we identify with as a separate entity in relationship with other equally separate beings and things and existing in an apparently linear historical time/space is an illusion. The ego-self is seen as an illusory compendium of physical and psychological aggregates manifested through the conditioned and conditioning law of cause and effect (karma). Because the nature of the ego-self is conditioned, it is therefore impermanent and subject to change and dissolution. This is not only true in the case of the ego-self but of the entire phenomenal and physical universe.

Because our mundane state of consciousness is dualistic, we are incapable in our ordinary day-to-day experience of apprehending this true state of existence, which can only be realized in profound states of meditation. This being the case, we cling to those things that endorse and reinforce the feeling of a permanent continuity of ego-self.

According to Buddhist teaching, this inability to recognize the actual nonexistence of the ego-self—while acknowledging its relative existence—binds us to a continual cycle of death and rebirth over incalculable eons of time, because the continually self-replicating patterns of conditioned and conditioning consciousness are ever reconstituting, without resolution. These repeatedly reincarnating lives are characterized by suffering and dissatisfaction due to our powerful attachment to things that are in themselves as impermanent and lacking in substantiality as the ego-self that clings to them.

What Buddhism teaches is a path that leads out of this existential cul-de-sac to the realization and experience of a higher, nondualistic state of consciousness, which completely revolutionizes one's state of being, finally resulting in liberation from the perpetual cycle of death and rebirth.

A few hundred years after the body-death of Sakyamuni Buddha, a schism occurred within the movement of early Buddhists, resulting in the emergence of two distinct schools. The first based itself on the original oral compilation and preservation of the Buddha's teachings (Dharma), known as the Hinyana or Theravada school, still the principle school in Southeast Asia. While the second, known as the Mahayana school, developed a much broader and more profound interpretation of the teachings based on revelations within the teachings that transcend the spoken and written word and taught in some sects (especially Zen) by way of direct transmission—mind-to-mind. The latter is the type of Buddhism found in Tibet, China, Mongolia, Korea, and Japan.

The term "Buddha" refers both to the Absolute as well as to beings who become enlightened through realization of the Absolute. The Mahayana school recognizes countless beings apart from the historical Buddha who have gained enlightenment in other world systems from beginningless time. While a primordial Buddha, or one that has attained supreme enlightenment, is referred to in the masculine, this is merely a convention, as this state of being transcends sex and gender.

folk nembutsu: It should be noted that in the story "Mr. Morishita's Treasure," we encounter the Nembutsu used by his aunt, as it is used in Japanese syncretic folk religions, as a magic spell, which has nothing to do with the true Nembutsu as described below.

Fudō-Myōō: Fudō-Myōō (Skt. Acalanātha). Regarded as a messenger of the Sun Buddha Dainichi Nyorai and depicted in wrathful aspect, holding a sword in one hand and a rope in the other and surrounded by a halo of flames.

haiku: A short seventeen-syllable poem, traditionally with a 5-7-5 syllable pattern and natural and seasonal references.

honji-suijaku: A theory by which the kami are understood as secondary manifestations of certain Buddhas and bodhisattvas. Buddhist temples and Shintō shrines shared the same compounds up until the Meiji era (1868–1912), as some still do to this day.

A few syncretic sects developed from this arrangement, one of the most interesting being Shugendō ("The Way of the Mountain"). The priests of this sect are called *yamabushi*, and they used to carry out severe ascetic practices in particular sacred mountains, which they understood as living mandalas. Though these practices are much diluted today, they were said to endue the priests with miraculous powers leading to enlightenment.

The doctrine of *suijaku* has led to a confusion in the minds of many Japanese up to the present; they find no difficulty in avowing faith in both systems of belief.

Jizō: A bodhisattva who liberates beings from the hell realms and is popularly regarded as a protector of travelers, women in childbirth, and the spirits of dead children. He is one of the most popular bodhisattvas in Japan, and small shrines (Jizō-dō) are found throughout the countryside, by roadsides, at the entrances to villages, and beside fields.

Jōdo Shin Sect: This sect represents the ultimate flowering of a school of Buddhism called the Pure Land School, which draws its main doctrine from three sutras in which the historical Buddha Sakyamuni describes the path for human beings in the decadent or "last dharmic age," called Mappo—an age of rampant materialism and spiritual degeneration. In it he describes how human beings no longer have the ability to bring about enlightenment through their own spiritual power and describes the need for dependence on the liberating grace of a Buddha called Amida [Skt. Amitābha and Amitāyus], who as a bodhisattva made a vow to liberate all sentient beings who meditated on him and invoked his Name, and resides in a pure land or paradise (i.e., a "Buddha field" without karmic obstacles) in the West.

The Jōdo Shin sect or True Pure Land sect, founded by Shinran, one of Japan's great geniuses of Buddhist thought in the thirteenth century whose teachings were mainly propagated through his writings, teaches single-minded reliance on just this practice of invoking the Name in the form of *Namu Amida Butsu*, which means to pay homage to and seek refuge in Amida Buddha. This practice is called the *nembutsu*, and through it an awareness of one's deep karmic sinfulness and inability to transcend it arises, leading to the development of complete and doubt-free entrusting in the Vow of this Buddha, a state of consciousness known as *shinjin*. Briefly, *shinjin* means the profound realization, while still remaining a human being filled with karmic evil, that one's true nature is the Mind of Amida Buddha. At this point, the *nembutsu* itself, becomes a spontaneous utterance of the Name of Amida and is experienced as a manifestation of the dynamic Mind (wisdom/ compassion) of this Buddha acting throughout the universe.

Kannon: Kannon [Skt. Avalokitesvara] Bodhisattva of compassion. In Japan and China, usually depicted in feminine aspect, and around whom a cult similar to the Mary cult in Europe arose.

Ryōkan: A Zen poet-priest (1758–1831). One of Japan's favorite poets. He led an itinerant life, begging and never settling anywhere permanently. He is famous for his innocent nature and his joy in playing with children.

Shingon Sect: This sect was one of the first to become established in Japan in the ninth century, along with the Tendai sect. It was founded by Kūkai (posthumously named Kōbō Daishi) after he returned from studying in China. The Shingon sect is one of the two esoteric or Tantric schools of Japanese Buddhism (the other being the Tendai sect), and its name is a translation of the Sanskrit word "mantra." The Buddha central to its practice is the great Cosmic Sun Buddha Dainichi Nyorai [Skt. Mahavairocana], and it teaches that the Absolute is present in all phenomena. In its practice it emphasizes the use of mantra, mandala, mudra (ritualized hand gestures symbolizing aspects of the Absolute), and dharini (verses similar to mantra, but longer). The object of practice is identification with a particular Buddha and the attainment of enlightenment in the present body.

The weakness in Shingon, however, is the danger of it degenerating into magical and superstitious practices.

Shintō: Shintō is the indigenous religion of the islands of Japan and has survived from the earliest times. Its continued existence to the present day, in spite of the introduction and popularity of Buddhism from the sixth century onward, is not only a testimony to the spiritual maturity of Buddhism itself and its tolerance of other beliefs but also to the Japanese people.

Central to Shintō is the concept of the kami, or gods. In fact the word "Shintō " itself means "The Way of the Gods," and while everything in the phenomenal universe is seen to be possessed of a divine spirit or kami, only those things or beings that exhibit extraordinary qualities or powers are singled out for actual veneration. The idea of kami, therefore, includes the personified powers of Nature wherein anything that gives an otherworldly or numinous ambiance or aura, or manifests in a particularly strange or unusual way, may be seen as either the abode of a kami or as a manifestation of the kami itself, such as caves, mountains, waterfalls, trees, rocks, winds, certain animals and birds, etc.—Nature understood as a bridge or conduit between the mundane world of humans and the realm of the divine. Human beings, also, who in their lives were in possession of unusual or extraordinary powers or gifts, are considered to be important kami after their deaths. In the past, of course, the emperor was venerated as a kami descended directly from the sun goddess Amaterasu Ōmikami. No moral considerations are applied to whether the powers or talents manifested are capable of creating good or evil, as long as they are prodigious. Great tyrants may be considered kami just as much as great heroes or poets, though the former may demand more in the way of propitiation! The ancestors, too, are treated as kami that are personal to and venerated by their families (though in Japan, because of the special syncretic relationship that existed in the past between Buddhism and Shintō, the ancestral kami are represented in the family Buddhist house-altar). The ancestors may have benign or malign influences on their living relatives, according to the conditions of their relationships with them during their lifetimes or whether the surviving relatives treat their graves and memories with the appropriate respect to their role as kami after their death.

Towns, villages, crafts, and trades all come under the tutelage of particular kami. In the case of a village, for example, it may be the deified ancestor of a local family who had been the lord of that area or the head of the local ruling clan, as in the case of Sora.

There is no moral law in Shintō per se, other than the maintenance of a harmonious balance mediated through a symbiotic relationship between human beings and kami. Purity is of the utmost importance, and birth, death, and blood are considered the greatest pollutants that desecrate areas sanctified by the presence of kami. It is in this idea of pollution that the only real concept of evil exists in the Shintō religion.

Festivals are held for the various kami, such as the kami of a village, when the kami is symbolically transferred to a portable shrine that is either transported on wheels or carried like a palanquin around the parish. Shops and houses are visited where offerings are made to the kami and blessings are bestowed upon businesses and households in turn. In this way the relationship between the kami and human beings is revitalized and the bonding of the people of the village strengthened.

The ground-energy of Shintō is the affirmation of life and is characterized by a potent vibrancy.

torii: Gateway to a Shintō shrine that is the demarcation between the mundane world of human beings and the sacred abode of a kami. It is constructed of two uprights with a long crossbeam resting across their tops. Just beneath it is a much shorter crossbeam that braces between the two uprights. It is generally constructed of wood (left unadorned, or lacquered vermilion in the case of *inari* or "fox shrines"), granite, bronze, or in some cases these days even concrete. The style varies slightly according to the period.

The meaning of the word *"torii"* is somewhat obscure, and no one I asked seemed to know, including shrine priests. The character for *torii* literally reads "bird perch." It has been suggested that this may refer to an incident in the creation myth of the Japanese archipelago in which the sun goddess hid in a cave and refused to come out, thus darkening the world. A cock is said to have landed on a perch outside the cave and crowed for her to come out. But whatever the origin, there is in the image, the suggestion of something that comes down out of the sky and perches on something that is firmly rooted in the earth. This gives the feeling of a celestial being or energy perhaps, coming down and uniting with a terrestrial one or simply taking on an earthly form.